Your Boss is an Idiot

Why things don't make sense to you at work

Eric Petracca

This book is an original publication by Eric Petracca.

This is a work of fiction. Names, characters, places, and incidents either are the product of the author's imagination or are used fictitiously, and any resemblance to actual persons, living or dead, business establishments, events, or locals is entirely coincidental.

Copyright © 2021, 2022 by Eric Petracca.
Text design and layout Eric Petracca.

All rights reserved.
This book, or parts thereof, may not be reproduced in any form without permission. The scanning, uploading, and distribution of this book via the Internet or via any other means without the permission of the publisher is illegal and punishable by law. Please purchase only authorized electronic editions, and do not participate in or encourage electronic piracy of copyrighted materials. Your support of the author's rights is appreciated.

First edition: 2021

To my coworkers, managers, and teams, thank you.

It's been a journey.

Eric

Most people are bad at their jobs.	1
Sometimes your best isn't good enough.	5
Just because it's simple doesn't mean it's easy.	7
It's like falling off a bicycle.	9
That's the job.	11
Anyone can hold it together for a year.	13
If you can't be right, be predictably wrong.	15
Once is a mistake. Twice is a problem.	17
If I have to do your job to get it done, I don't need you.	19
Never apologize.	21
Don't blame the job, blame the job fit.	25
A problem always has at least two solutions.	27
Innovate yourself out of a job.	29
Look for the opportunity to time travel.	33
People get away with the least amount of effort.	37
Not no risk, no unknown risk.	41
If more than one person is responsible, no one is responsible.	45
If you don't do the things you are responsible to do, who will?	47
Even a little light is enough to see by.	49
Some people are tall. Some people are short.	51
Most people need the job they have.	55

You are not perfect.	57
They have a job (and so do you).	61
Email is the devil.	65
If no one is running the meeting, you run the meeting.	69
Everyone is telling a story.	73
That's because you are a superhero.	75
Repeat yourself.	77
Be clear and concise.	79
Give every person your absolute peak performance, but…	81
You're supposed to be busy.	85
This isn't rocket surgery.	87
We're not building rockets.	89
It's like spraying for spiders.	91
Your job is to decide who you are not going to make happy.	95
One thing in the morning. One thing in the afternoon.	97
Do what you can do.	99
The difference between 0 and 1 is infinity.	103
The knife cuts both ways.	107
If you want to outrun the devil, start by tying your shoes.	109
Your glasses are always in the last place you look…	113
New Line Dancers Go to the Middle	115
Do the last thing you want to do.	119

Have a plan, work a plan.	121
Every incentive program is also a disincentive program.	123
There are a lot of lists you do not want to be on.	127
You are not a bad person. You just need more practice.	129
Don't be right, do right.	131
No one is out to get you.	133
What happens behind the counter stays behind the counter.	135
Make it look easy.	137
Email is not your job.	139
People hear only what they want to hear.	141
Most people do not understand what it is supposed to look like.	143
Most people don't understand that they are the problem.	145
Nobody cares about your problems.	147
If it was easy, it would already be done.	149
There is always a finite amount of risk.	151
Give the Benefit of the Doubt.	155
Have excellent conversations.	157
Give them a way out.	159
Find the edges so you can find the middle.	163
Execute is in the name!	165
The World is a Big Place.	167
Ideas are easy. Execution is difficult.	169

There's always a #1 concern.	**171**
Offer to help.	**173**
We fill our days.	**175**
Things get better when you make them get better.	**177**
Don't manufacture drama.	**179**
Your words coming out of their mouths.	**181**
Every job has a purpose.	**183**
When you get what you want, stop talking.	**185**
Something always has to give.	**187**
Be the shadow, then be the light.	**189**
Braces make your teeth straight.	**191**
Most people don't do the thing they are good at…	**193**
Effort does not get results.	**195**
What worked yesterday won't work tomorrow.	**197**
There's a difference between blame and responsibility.	**199**
Be the Boss You Wish You Had	**201**

Who is this book for?

You (if you are already an executive)
This book is a collection of guidelines that were hard won from years of working with people throughout my career. If you're already an executive, I don't expect you'll find any of this surprising. What I do think this book will do for you is give you a new anchor point for how to think about these principles. Think of them like touchstones that bring you back to what matters in the moment. A simple turn of phrase can be a great way to remind yourself of what you already know you should be doing.

You (if you want to be an executive)
Making the jump from whatever you are doing now to taking on an executive role can be a big one. Some people learn from their own mistakes. Some people learn from other people's mistakes. Be the second kind of person. This book is full of stuff I learned along my career journey. I wish I had this book when I was starting out. It's dangerous to go alone. Take this.

You (if you think your boss is an idiot)
I'm going to level with you. Chances are good that your boss *is an idiot*. But let's assume for the rest of this book that your boss is not an idiot. Let's assume that the real problem is that the way you think about things at work is not the way your boss thinks about those same things. By the end of this ride, you might have a completely different understanding of why your boss does things the way they do them. Don't get the wrong idea. Your boss might still be an idiot. But at least they won't be a *nonsensical* idiot.

Most people are bad at their jobs.

This isn't going to sit well with most of you. But hear me out.

Think about the last time you got truly outstanding service from anyone in any field. Your doctor. Your dentist. Your mechanic. Your barista. Your massage therapist. Your employees. Your boss. Think about the last time a product impressed you - really knocked you off your feet. The build-quality. The sound. The feel. The design. It's rare. World-class performance is rare. Why?

Because if it was easy, it would already be done.

50% of the people you see driving around on the streets are in the bottom half of people with driving skills. 50% of the doctors you go to are in the bottom half of people with those medical skills. This isn't hyperbole. This is math. And this is true where you work, too. Even for the people who are above 50%, the next 35% of those people are only slightly better than average, but not great. It's not until you get into the top 15% and really the top 5% people you start to see incredible performance.

By definition, most of the people you interact with fall far below world-class in whatever they do. Again, consider the chances that the people you work with are the best in their field. Unless you are world-class yourself, it's not likely that you are working with world-class people. That's true for everyone you interact with at work or in your personal life.

Most people are just *meh*.

I'm not saying that people aren't trying to be great. People practice. People get experience with whatever they are doing the more they do it. But sometimes your best just isn't good enough. No amount of practice is going to make me into an Olympic swimmer. Expecting that everyone you work with can be the equivalent of an Olympic swimmer is delusional.

This principle isn't about putting people down. It is about understanding why your expectations aren't being met. It's also about recognizing that it is very likely that you are not meeting the expectations of others.

Consider that the person making your coffee probably stayed up too late playing video games or studying for a test, came in to work barely on time, nearly got in an accident on the way to work, and then parked too close to another car in the parking lot and had to shimmy out. They bumped the car next to them ever so gently and now there is a ding in the paint on the edge of the car they are borrowing from their roommate. They are "at work," but their heart is not in it. You can see this being the case, right?

Now imagine that it's not your barista we are talking about but your surgeon. And you are about to get a triple-bypass surgery.

This is real. All of those people around you are real. They have life and struggles. They are *dealing with things.* For you to not understand this or to expect something different from the people you work with is on you. The result is that most people (including you) are bad at their jobs.

Sometimes your best isn't good enough.

I originally saw this on a "demotivational" poster. It was meant as a joke. It is funny, in a way. But when I saw it, I realized that it is true!

My life changed at that moment.

Sometimes you give it your all and still come up short. Despite your best efforts, you fail. The number of times I've heard, "I'm trying my best," is ridiculous. We don't hire people for their best. We hire people to produce specific outcomes. If a desired outcome is not produced, I couldn't care less if you did your best because *your best isn't good enough*.

Before you get all high and mighty, this principle applies to *you too*. I'm as guilty as the next person of saying, "I'm trying!" Great. We are all trying. Trying is the *bare minimum*. Recognizing that your 100% sometimes doesn't get the job done is how we start to figure out what to do next.

This isn't about beating anyone up for poor performance. It's about honest conversations with the people you work with when someone falls short. Are your expectations too high? Are your desired outcomes only achievable by world-class performance? If so, remember that most people are bad at their jobs. But if your expectations are reasonable, the focus should not be on effort. The focus should be on results.

Trying your best is a crutch. It stops us from identifying the real problem for missed expectations. Saying, "You hired me to do a job. I put together a strategy that I thought would get us there. I put all of my effort into it, but it wasn't enough. Even upon reflection, there is nothing I could have done better than what I did. Those were my best efforts. Where do we go from here?" That course at least opens the door to a conversation about expectations management.

Just because it's simple doesn't mean it's easy.

Lots of things are simple. Most things are simple. But almost nothing is easy. That's an important, but subtle distinction. It affects us at work almost every day in a couple of key ways.

When you look at what someone else is supposed to get done, it almost always looks simple. If you find yourself saying things like, "You just do X," or, "I don't understand what the problem is," that's because from the outside almost everything looks simple. But almost nothing is easy. If it was easy it would already be done.

People are good at getting the easy stuff done. That's why there usually isn't a bunch of really easy stuff left for people to work on. It's usually only the difficult stuff left to do. But this has more to do with what we think of as "simple" and how we conflate the concept with what we think of as "easy."

Conceptually, landing a person on the moon is simple. You build a rocket. Aim at the moon. Blast off. Wait for a while. And then you're there. See? Simple. But of course we know that landing a person on the moon is not at all easy. There are literally a million little things that have to be carefully considered before even attempting something like this. To a lesser degree, that's what is happening at work all day long. Conceptually simple things are being worked on that are not at all easy to accomplish.

Be careful with oversimplifications. Describing things simply can be helpful for clarifying what needs to be accomplished to meet the goal. But when it crosses over from being a helpful clarification to sounding like you've made something simple into something easy, you've crossed the line.

It's like falling off a bicycle.

You never forget how to do it.

If you remember learning to ride a bicycle, there's a good chance you remember falling off at least once. It's quite a feeling. Depending on how big of a risk-taker you are, the fall might have even left a permanent mark.

Work is like that. You will learn stuff. You will try new things. It will be uncomfortable. You will fall off the bicycle.

Everyone will tell you that you never forget how to *ride* a bicycle. That might be true. It might not be true. But one thing that is true no matter what is that you will never forget how to *fall off* a bicycle. Why? Because that's the default state. If you make a big enough mistake riding the bike, you fall off.

Why am I telling you this?

Because that's the default state at work, too. If you make a big enough mistake, you *fall off*. You overcorrect. You lose balance. The trick is knowing how to fall off. There are good ways to fall off and bad ways to fall off. Get to know the difference.

By all means, practice riding the bike. That's what's going to get you from one place to another. But if you know the default state is to fall off when you make a mistake, get good at falling off. There are ways to crash the bike that minimize the carnage. The same is true for you at work.

That's the job.

In college, I was interested in a lot of different things. I took a lot of different classes, including senior accounting.

Senior accounting was the class designed for accounting majors, for people who wanted to go on to accounting as a career. I didn't have those career designs, but I did like how accounting worked and I wanted to learn more.

We were nearing the end of term and the professor assigned a group project that was a large part of our final grade. Me, a humanities major, and three other students, all accounting majors, had to perform an audit on a fictional company. We were sitting in the library around a table for the umpteenth hour, poring over financial statements and transaction records when the grumbling started.

One of the people in my group - an accounting major - turned to us and started complaining that the project was tedious and boring. The other students piled on. It might have been the coffee talking, but I was blown away.

I said, "hey, you know this is the job, right?"

"That's the job. What we're doing right now, this is what the job is. You will be doing this, or something like this, every single day of your working life."

The same thing will happen to you at some point in your career. The idea of the job and the execution of the job are two different things.

My dream job is to be chief ice cream taster.

The idea of tasting ice cream all day sounds wonderful. I can't imagine anything better. And yet, I've never met an ice cream taster. When I really think about it, I'll bet it's awful to be an ice cream taster. By definition, I would be tasting the worst ice cream flavors all the time. I would be tasting poorly executed ice cream flavors and trying to make a distinction between a slightly sweeter vanilla and a slightly less sweet vanilla.

But...

That's the job.

Anyone can hold it together for a year.

It's the second year where things start to fall apart.

Over the course of your career, you'll hire a lot of people. You'll work with a lot of people. You'll have a lot of bosses. You'll have a lot of employees. Companies get bigger and smaller. Departments reorganize. New products are developed. You'll have opportunities to move up and to move on.

Everyone says that they want to hit the ground running. And everyone does, sort of. Not really in the way that we mean, but they are running. A million people expect the new person to get up to speed quickly, figure out what they are supposed to be doing, and basically just fit right into whatever culture, process, and systems you have already working.

We all say that we want to hear the new person's perspective. We say it because it sounds good. But there's almost always a reason why you do what you do. It may not be a good reason, but there's a reason.

Depending on the position, some people are expected to get up to speed quickly. If it's a routine task-focused position and the person is there to perform a specific function, it's reasonable to expect them to get on the ball. Or if the position is based on mostly transferable skills, there's a more gentle learning curve. But for the positions that start flirting with management or strategy, wrong moves can really derail whatever the company is working on.

For those positions, you don't want someone to come in and start breaking things.

In practice, this means that a new high-level manager is expected to "do nothing" for quite a while. They can lean on months of "listening" and "learning" and "getting the lay of the land" before people start to ask what they are actually doing. Things tend to go well for the first year because unless something is truly broken, people tend to come to work and do whatever the job is that they are there to do. Sometimes teams will even naturally perform better simply because the new boss isn't in the way!

By the end of the first year, the new boss isn't really new anymore. There's a certain pressure to start moving the strategy forward. And that usually means changing things. This is where the leader gets tested. Did they build relationships? Do they have the skills to build consensus? How are they at managing change?

The second year gets rough. The boss can no longer lean on listening and learning. They need to start doing and changing. It's a different skill set. And one that quite frankly they were hired for in the first place.

If you can't be right, be predictably wrong.

You can't be right 100% of the time. No one can.

Once you accept that, you are also accepting the fact that you will be *wrong* some of the time.

Be *predictably* wrong.

When you have a framework for making decisions, you will have ample opportunity to test that framework. Throughout your work day, you will put your framework to the test as you approach problems. As you go, think to yourself, "there's a chance that I'm wrong."

This isn't to stop you from moving forward. This isn't to make you second-guess your decisions. This is to understand that being wrong is part of the process. Your goal is to make that wrongness consistent, measurable, and predictable.

This sounds weird. It sounds weird because no one *wants to be wrong*. But you *will be* wrong sometimes. Every time you are wrong, figure out why you were wrong. Wrongness is a predictable outcome based on how you approach your work process.

When something goes wrong, rather than just chalk It up to random chance, evaluate the circumstances. What caused it to happen?

This matters because something *did cause you to be wrong*. There is a flaw in your process. The real question is this: Was the wrongness predictable?

Because if it was predictable, you could have done something about it.

Here's the secret: Most wrongness *is predictable*.

If you start looking at all the things that go wrong throughout your work day, you can begin to categorize the causes. You'll notice the patterns. You'll see how mistakes happen and when they happen. It's spooky.

Once these wrong outcomes are predictable, you can begin to avoid them. It all starts with being predictably wrong.

Once is a mistake. Twice is a problem.

Everyone makes mistakes. Even you.

Sometimes a mistake is so egregious that it can't be overlooked. It can't be viewed as a learning opportunity. But that's rare. That takes a special kind of mistake. For the run-of-the-mill mistakes that happen all the time, most people learn from them and move on. They either don't make that mistake again or if they do, it's super rare.

Then there's the other kind of person.

You know the one. You probably work with someone like this. They make mistakes. They may even be able to admit that they make mistakes. But they make the same mistakes over and over.

Something goes wrong, someone misses something important, an error occurs, the ball gets dropped. It's not great but it happens. It's when the same mistake happens again that things *should* get interesting.

Before I go on, let's make it clear what I mean by mistake. If your job is to catch footballs that are being thrown at you, it's not a mistake when you don't complete the catch. Missing a catch is part of the job. You're shooting for high percentages for catching the football, but it's not reasonable to expect that anyone catches the football 100% of the time.

Your job is like that, too. It may not be as clear as catching footballs, but there's some aspect of your job where you'll "miss the catch," possibly on a regular basis. By all means, improve in that area, but that's not a mistake.

A mistake is when you do something wrong that you could have avoided if you did it right. It's when something happens that shouldn't have happened. You missed a deadline that you could have hit if you had a better plan. You avoided working on something because you procrastinated and it turned out to be more important than you understood. That kind of thing.

If you do something like that once, it's a mistake.

If you do it again, it's a problem.

It's a problem because you should have known better. You had direct experience that you didn't put into action. Refusal to learn from your mistakes is *always* a problem.

If I have to do your job to get it done, I don't need you.

This one confuses a lot of people.

Everyone has a job to do. Most people don't understand what that job is, but it still needs to be done even if you don't understand what it is.

My job as a manager is to make the desired outcomes *understandable*. Your job is to make those desired outcomes *a reality*. If I have to do your job, then by definition *I don't need you*.

I'm being blunt on purpose.

Have this conversation with your boss. Ask if you are meeting the objectives of the job. Most bosses have not been confronted this way and are bad at describing exactly what those outcomes are for your job. But it's a place to start.

Most of us are not clearly told what we are supposed to be accomplishing. We're left to guess at it. We usually find out the hard way that we didn't meet the goal. We usually find out exactly what the goal was after it is too late. Don't be caught in that situation.

If you're in charge, your job is to literally set the objectives for the positions that report to you. Make it clear. And make it clear when the job isn't being completed. If the objectives are not being met, it should never be a surprise. It's not a secret you want to keep. Be direct about performance.

Why?

Many people in charge operate under the assumption that the people working for them know what they want them to accomplish. They don't. Trust me. It's like finding out if the stove is on by touching it. This isn't about punishment or praise. This is about simply describing the desired outcome.

This seems so simple. But think about your own career, your own experience with your supervisors. Have they always been clear about objectives? Have you ever been surprised at a performance evaluation? Have you ever found out the hard way that you didn't measure up? Yeah. That's all happened to you, hasn't it? There's a really good chance that you are doing the exact same thing to the people who work for you now! Not sure? Ask them.

Never apologize.

This isn't hyperbole. I mean it. Never say you are sorry at work.

Should you admit that you are wrong when you are? Absolutely.

Should you offer solutions when you've screwed something up? Absolutely.

What you shouldn't do is say that you are "sorry."

Sorry for what?

Sorry it happened? Sorry you messed up? Sorry it didn't work out the way you planned? Sorry you got caught?

Sorry doesn't mean anything. It's not a solution. It doesn't move us forward.

The reality is that you are screwing up things all day long. We all are. We're missing things. We're sending the wrong messages. We're offending people. We're being pulled in twenty different directions. We're letting people down in ways we can't fathom. We're disappointing *ourselves*.

Can you feel remorse for all of these things? I guess. I mean, most of the time you don't even know you are doing it. You're just trying to get through the day.

In other words, you're either apologizing for things that don't matter, not apologizing for things that do matter, or when things have gone obviously wrong you're apologizing for things when what you should be doing is getting to work on solutions.

Track yourself at work. Are you apologizing all day long? Did you forget to unmute your phone on a conference call then *apologized to everyone for the slight delay* after you figured it out? Have you heard someone else do this?

Did you think to yourself, "That person is genuinely sorry for stealing five seconds from me when they forgot to unmute. I'm so pleased and will forgive them immediately. How polite and endearing."? Probably not.

We start leaning on all these little apologies throughout the workday like a crutch. Don't do it.

It's especially infuriating when something does go sideways to have the person responsible for it in my office apologizing. By all means, take responsibility. But "sorry" is for children. What do you expect me to do with your apology?

There's another side to this that's important to point out. Your perception of what went wrong is often very different from the perception of everyone else. If you are responsible for something that went wrong, your ability to identify the problem, propose a solution, then execute it is valuable. Things get messed up all the time. Fixing those things and moving forward is the job. Apologizing is about blame and consequences. That's not where you want to focus. And it's not where you want everyone else to focus. It doesn't solve anything.

Stop apologizing. Start solving.

Don't blame the job, blame the job fit.

Jobs exist because work needs to be done. This isn't a charity.

The number of times I hear someone complaining that, "this job sucks," is way too high. The job is the job. You aren't going to change the job to make it "not suck" because the job doesn't exist *for you*. The job exists because someone needs something done. They are willing to pay for it. Are you willing to do that work for that pay?

If it was fun, it wouldn't be a job. We have a different word for that. *Play.*

So don't blame the job if you don't like it.

But don't get me wrong: some jobs do suck.

They suck *for you*.

If your job sucks, it's because the job is a bad fit. You don't fit well with that job. It's not for you. You're not for it.

Due to a bunch of life circumstances, people end up with the wrong job all the time. And they can't get out. They are stuck in the wrong job. And it sucks. *For them.*

That same job does not suck *for someone else*.

The trap is when you start thinking that the job is the problem when the real problem is the job *fit*. If you aren't a good fit for that job, you will have problems with it. But realizing that the fit is the problem gives you a whole lot more options for possible solutions.

Blaming the job doesn't give you options because the job is simply asking you to do some work, some way, for some pay. That's it. When you accept that it might not be the job *for you*, you can look for opportunities to find a job that is for you. Accepting it is the first step.

A problem always has at least two solutions.

The second solution is to quit.

I find this statement freeing. Whenever I run into a problem that seems impossible, I remember that there's always another way.

I may not like the other solution. I may not like *the consequences* of quitting. But there is always that option.

It's easy to get focused on the impossible problem. And that focus can lock you in to one way of thinking. The path that gets you from where you are to what needs to be accomplished may seem impossible, but the real problem is that you are focusing on that one path. Remembering that you can always quit means that there's always another way. If there's one other way, there might be others.

Looking for more solutions is easier when you know that at least one other solution already exists.

Innovate yourself out of a job.

...and into a new one.

I'm lazy.

So are you.

But the difference is that I am *motivated* by my laziness.

I spend my time figuring out how to get my work done without me doing it.

And I don't mean pushing work off onto other people. This isn't about avoiding work. This isn't about slacking off. This is the age-old adage of working smarter rather than harder.

We've all heard some version of this advice at some point in our lives. Work smarter not harder! It's usually when we are young and doing something and someone more experienced shows us an "easier" way to do it.

Most of us see the easier way, give it a try, shrug, and that's it. Yep, that's easier. You start doing it the easier way and move on.

I do that. Except I don't move on. I find the smarter way for every single thing I do.

In other words, I don't care what my job description says. I never have. My *real job* is to innovate myself out of that job and into another one.

My goal at every job I've ever had is to figure out how to get everything done *without anyone needing to do it*.

Stop looking at the work in front of you. Start thinking about how the work gets done. All day long you are doing things that either don't need to be done or can be done a better way. This stuff is relatively easy to see when you are looking at an assembly line. Parts come in, get worked on, and go back out. If you can shave a few seconds off here and there, it starts to add up. It's obvious.

Guess what?

The same thing is true at your job, even if you don't work on an assembly line. Those seconds matter. They add up.

It's just more difficult to see if you don't work on an assembly line.

You likely have a lot of autonomy at your job. It might not feel like it, but you do. What you don't have is any incentive to improve your work process. You are likely paid to work for a certain amount of *time*. As long as your output is above the acceptable amount, you'll keep getting a paycheck.

The worry is that if you innovate yourself out of a job, you'll be *out of a job*. The reality is that it doesn't work this way. There is always more work to do. This mindset of innovation carries over to the way everyone you work with sees you. It is dynamic and interesting.

A lot of people do a job for a while, get good at it, then get promoted when their boss leaves. They start doing the boss' job, maybe get good at it, then get promoted again. At some point, they get stuck. Why? Because getting good at the job you have is intrinsically limiting. There's only so much you can do to get good at *that* job.

Instead, get good at innovation. Your current job - whatever it is - is only a platform to demonstrate your skills at improving the job. It's not you that's improving *at that job*. It's you who's *improving the job itself*. You aren't learning how to be a better whatever-it-is. That will always end up with you getting stuck. Instead, make the whatever-it-is better. This approach keeps the door open forever to new opportunities.

It takes practice. Sit beside yourself at work. Ask yourself, "What am I doing and why?" Be aware of how things are taking your attention, how you spend your time. How much of your time is taken by things that are simply there to fill in the day? Start there. What could you do with that time if you reclaimed it and moved it into a single block for the day or week?

Look for the opportunity to time travel.

There will be times in your career where you are responsible for executing a strategy, or part of a strategy. Either way, it's easy to become focused on the timelines and plans and miss the opportunity to skip forward and get to the same outcome.

Time travel.

I call it time traveling because you end up in "the future" but you skip all the time it would normally take to get there.

Many of you will read this and be thinking *of course you should look for shortcuts that make sense and still deliver the desired outcome.* Yes, you're right you *should* do that. But that's not what I'm talking about.

When there is more than one person involved in making a decision, there's almost always consensus thinking. Remember, compromise is when two people don't get what they want. We're told that compromise is a good thing because it's how we move things forward. This is true. But it is the *consequence* of working with other people, not the *goal*.

Think of it this way: If two people had the same idea, the same goal, and the same way to accomplish that goal, there would be no need to compromise. Both people would get what they want. In that scenario, compromise isn't lauded as the ideal because it's not needed. It's when something about the idea, the goal, or the approach differs between the two that a compromise needs to be reached.

In almost every case, you will need to compromise to accomplish the goals of the organization. Heck, just setting the goals and strategy involves compromise. Being good at compromise is part of the job. But don't pretend that compromise is anything more than the result of giving up on what *you want* to get something done.

This means that when you are reading the strategic plan of the organization, you are looking at compromise after compromise. At every point along the way, every single person involved in creating and executing the strategy didn't get exactly what they wanted. They *compromised*.

Why is this important to understand?

As a leader, your job is to execute the strategic plan with full knowledge that it is likely not what you would do and not the way you would do it. And that's true for every single person you are leading, too!

Even if it's your company, 100% owned by you, built from the ground up, you will always, always need to compromise to get anything done. You probably don't believe me.

Imagine that you make a product. You make all the choices. You bring it to market. How much do you want to charge for that product?

The rational answer is... All the money in the world.

How much will you actually charge for that product?

Exactly as much as the market will pay.

See? Compromise.

What does this have to do with time travel?

If you accept that the strategic plan is full of compromise, it's easier to see that what happens when executing the plan is that people get focused on the *plan* and not the *strategy*. We spend a lot of time "checking in" with other people, motivating, measuring, creating milestones, putting projects into place, making presentations, coordinating meetings, and setting outcomes, that we forget that there's a point to all of this. The strategy is ultimately about achieving a specific outcome. The rest of it is just the stuff that gets you there. It's also the stuff that gets in the way of getting you there.

Do not miss the opportunity to refocus on the outcome, the point, of the strategic plan. Why is executing the plan important? If that's your focus, you can often bypass a lot of the work that is the result of the compromise required to put that strategic plan into place.

People get away with the least amount of effort.

People are not lazy. They are practical. They do what they can *get away* with.

When you look around you at work, at your co-workers, your boss, teammates, vendors, and everyone else in your organization, what you are seeing is people doing the least amount required to get through the day.

You're probably thinking that you work really hard. It's all those other people who are slackers.

You're probably right.

I'm not saying that you are a slacker. I'm not saying you aren't getting your job done. But everyone is doing what you are doing. Really!

Everyone you work with is doing exactly as much work as is required to continue employment. You are surrounded by people who continue to work for the organization. By definition, they are doing the job.

Could they do better? Sure.

Could *you* do better? You bet.

But are you doing good enough to keep your job? Well, yes. You know this is true because you still have your job.

What happens if you do more or better than the job that's required of you?

You get a promotion.

Do some people get a promotion without working harder? Maybe. But they did something that got them a promotion. It may not be something that appears valuable to you or that matters in your opinion, but whatever it was worked for them.

In other words, everyone you work with has been promoted to whatever level of work and value they can provide and then stopped there. Maybe they are still learning and growing and will work toward another promotion. But for now, that's where they are.

If I worked hard in the past, went for extra training, put in extra hours, worked on processes, demonstrated my value and then received a promotion, I'm now in a position that requires that level of knowledge and experience to perform the functions of the job. Unless I do more, work even harder, learn more, then I am - by definition - doing the least amount required to keep my current job.

There's nothing wrong with this. It's just the way it is. For everyone. Including you.

If you are working extra hard to get ahead, that's why it feels like everyone else is lazy. But they aren't. They are just being practical. They have a different goal than you do. They want to maintain employment. You want a promotion.

Once you stop working harder for a promotion, *you become them*.

Not no risk, no unknown risk.

Some people say they are risk-takers. They wear it like a badge of honor.

I don't have a problem with taking risks. Taking risks is how we create value. Risk and reward are two sides of the same coin.

Think of it this way: If you could figure out a way to do business without risk and produce income, someone would already be doing that. Taking risk is how you produce income, no matter what business you are in.

Everyone is a risk-taker. It's just that most people don't understand how to evaluate risk. So, what you end up with are people who take outrageous risks that sometimes pay off. Of course big risks will occasionally pay off. And what happens when they do? You hear about it.

In other words, you are more likely to hear about the person who took the big risk and it paid off than the thousand other people who took the big risk and lost everything.

This makes sense, right?

And it warps our understanding of how much risk is really out there.

The problem isn't risk. Risk is required to produce value. The problem is *unknown* risk.

The risk you don't know about is what sneaks up on you. Get good at evaluating risk.

Once you are good at evaluating risk, you can start to make more measured plans that produce the expected amount of value. The risk/reward relationship will be predictable and reasonable.

Get ready to be called a person who doesn't take risks.

The person who shows up every day, understands risk, and carefully moves the business forward doesn't get the big story. They aren't being reckless. People enjoy the spectacle. Sometimes, the story of someone who took a big risk and crashed isn't even told as a cautionary tale.

How many times have you heard that you need to take risks to get ahead?

A million times.

Heck, I said it just a few paragraphs ago.

The difference is that when other people say it, it's usually after they failed spectacularly and they are trying to spin it into a success. Usually, the person telling you that story took another big risk and this time it paid off. Otherwise, why would you be listening to their story? The story of someone who keeps trying big things and failing isn't interesting until they succeed.

But it is a lot more interesting than the story of the person who understands the risks they are taking and turns each one into a small success. No one wants to hear that story.

Guess which approach works most of the time?

The boring one.

Be boring.

No unknown risks.

If more than one person is responsible, no one is responsible.

I'll bet you've been part of this little party before. Your boss sends out an email with instructions to do something, but instead of sending the email to one person the email has everyone on your team in the TO: line.

Not a fun party.

What's the problem here?

Most of the people on the team will look at the email, assume it's for someone else, and then ignore it. At best, all it did was distract them from what they were supposed to be doing. A few people on the team will assume that the email is for someone else, but that the other person isn't going to do it. So, they take on the task. It gets done, but it bothers them and they get resentful. Someone on the team is actually the person who should be working on the task. Sometimes they even know it's supposed to be them. But because the email is sent to everyone, it's sent to no one. They know that the busy do-gooders on the team will pick up the slack and get it done anyway.

The thing gets done (usually).

That's the worst part. The boss throws things out there by sending an email and lets the chips fall. Usually this works.

But it's confusing and costly. It impacts the team negatively by either wasting time, creating bitterness, or allowing people to avoid the work they should be doing.

What should happen?

The boss should assign the task to a specific person.

This seems easy, right? And it is. The person in charge needs to actually do their job. We don't call 'em managers for nothing. Start managing.

If you don't do the things you are responsible to do, who will?

Guess what? You have a job to do. So does everyone else.

Shocker.

Yet, I see people get this wrong all the time. Frequently, they are trying to do everyone else's job and not doing their own.

This is the double-whammy of feeling overworked and still not getting anything done. It burns you out. And managers are notoriously bad at helping you solve this problem because you are bailing them out of doing their job while you're at it.

Wait, what?

That's right. If you do someone else's job, a bad manager (which is almost all managers) will let you get away with it for a long time. Why? Because at the end of the day the work is getting done. It's easy for them to turn a blind eye to *how* it's getting done.

So, not only are you enabling your boss to do a bad job, but you're enabling your coworker to do a bad job. And since you are the responsible one, you're heaping pressure on yourself to get your own job done at the same time. Boom. Overworked. Underappreciated. Bitter. Angry. Depressed.

Does that sound familiar?

Flip this situation around. Let's assume you are the manager. Your job is to manage your team. That means you should be actively looking for performers who are taking up the slack. Plenty of people are more than happy to allow someone else to do the work for them. I guarantee you that this is happening on your team right now.

On your team, right now, someone is doing someone else's job. And you are letting it happen because the work is getting done. Why rock the boat?

Because it's your job.

If you don't manage your team, who will? That's literally your job. The person you are allowing to take up the slack is the one who is overworked, underappreciated, bitter, angry, and depressed. Because you aren't doing your job.

In other words, your best employee is almost always going to be the one who feels the worst because you aren't doing your job.

The fix is easy. Do your job.

Don't let anyone on your team get away with not doing the work they need to be doing. And, importantly, don't let anyone on your team do the work that someone else should be doing. The knife cuts both ways.

Even a little light is enough to see by.

Have you ever had the experience of being in a completely dark room? A room where there is no light at all? It's eerie. But if you add even just a little bit of light, it changes the entire experience. It takes almost no light to be able to see in a dark space.

Everything is like that.

When you are at work, there will be times you feel stuck in a dark space. It could be a project that isn't going well or a boss that just isn't quite making sense. It could be a difficult coworker or new training program. Whatever it is, remember that even a little light can show you the way out.

I spend my time looking for that little bit of light. It's there. It's always there.

I have a dark mood by nature. I don't think it came from anywhere special. I have nothing to complain about. By most measures, I live a charmed existence. I'm fortunate. Blessed, even. And yet, it's easy for me to find the worst in a situation.

I know this about myself. So, to balance this out, I've practiced saying one good thing or offering one alternative for any situation that looks like it's all bad. This is the classic "finding the silver lining" play.

We've all heard that every dark cloud has a silver lining.

Have you tried actually looking for it?

It takes practice.

It also freaks people out.

Them: "Bob's late to work today."
Me: "Maybe he met the love of his life on the way in."

Them: "We're going to be up all night working on this."
Me: "We never really get the chance to talk, so this will be a good opportunity to catch up."

Them: "My car broke down and I had to call for a ride."
Me: "Maybe you avoided an accident."

Over and over. There's always at least one possible explanation that is more positive or has a better outcome. Find it. Say it outloud.

People will stop complaining to you because they know that you aren't buying what they are selling. They know that you'll find the good in the bad situation. The complaints will start to leave your own mind, too.

If you're in a dark place, practice looking for the light switch instead of complaining about how dark it is.

Some people are tall. Some people are short.

This is a weird one.

It's weird because it's so blatantly obvious with physical characteristics like being tall or short. Tall people can see on top of the refrigerator. They don't have to think about it or do anything special. They just look over and there it is: the top of the refrigerator. Short people can't see on top of the refrigerator without help. They need a ladder or a mirror or a boost. Or they need to be strong enough to push the refrigerator over.

This seems silly to point out, right?

Except it's not silly to point out because people act all the time like everyone is the same when they clearly are not.

I'll take a moment here to say that this isn't about inequality or working toward equity. I'm talking about real differences between people that affect their ability at work to achieve a goal. The same way that I'm not going to be a successful professional basketball player because I'm simply not tall enough, there are a lot of other qualities that affect a person's ability to be successful in many jobs.

I'm not going to be a competitive powerlifter. I'm not built for it. I'm not going to be an Olympic sprinter. I'm not built for it. I'm also not going to be a great computer programmer. Could I take the classes and sit through the projects and write some software? Probably. Could I do it day in and day out as my career? Nope. *I'm not built for it.*

Somehow this is obvious and acceptable when it comes to crushing my dreams to play professional basketball, but is outrageous to suggest when someone is thinking about what career they should pursue. It doesn't need to be this way.

It's on all of us to take a hard look at what we bring to the table and find jobs that we can do and enjoy and where we can succeed. The number of times I've coached an employee who wants to move into management or an executive role, but who lacks any of the qualities to succeed in that role is astounding.

I'll bet you bristled when you read that last sentence.

There's an idea floating around out there that people can be anything they want to be if they just work hard enough.

Nope.

Sometimes your best isn't good enough.

You'll readily accept that I cannot be a professional basketball player because I'm not tall enough. But if I suggest that someone might not be cut out for an executive management role, I'm suddenly the bad guy.

Ultimately, only you can know if you can do the job that you set out to do. I'm not saying that you should let anyone stop you from trying. What I'm saying is that people have this idea that they will bend the job to their own limitations. That's rarely how it works. If you can make that work, that's a superpower unto itself that most people do not possess.

For the rest of us mere mortals, whatever job you want will come with a certain set of demands that you must be able to consistently meet to be successful. Sometimes these jobs will even come with prerequisites you'll need to meet to *even get the chance* to be successful.

If you want to be a professional basketball player, you will almost certainly need to be tall. Really tall. If you want to be an analyst, you will almost certainly need to be able to quickly digest large volumes of data, find patterns, describe those patterns, and provide useful commentary on how those patterns can be exploited. That's the job. If you can't do that, or can't imagine doing that all day every day, that's not the job for you. You're too "short" for it. Find something where you are the "tall" person.

The job you should be doing is waiting for you on top of the refrigerator.

Most people need the job they have.

Not everyone. But most people aren't working for fun. They need the paycheck.

Most of the people you work with have house payments and kids, retirement plans, vacations, credit card bills, new cars, expensive hobbies, and big dreams.

A vanishingly small number of people have the financial freedom to walk away from the job they have. Some might job-hop from one company to another for a better opportunity. But it's rare that someone doesn't need to work.

I'm not saying that people aren't there to do a good job. I'm just saying that you need to consider the motivation.

Most people are running at 110% of what they can afford.

Even though they can technically move from the job they have to another company for a better opportunity, the risk to do so if the transition doesn't work out keeps them rooted.

In other words, it's more than people just needing a job. They need *that* job. They need the job they already have.

Think about all of your meetings, coaching sessions, presentations, and interactions with your coworkers. The backdrop of every one of those things is that almost everyone shares the same foundational motivation: they need the job they have.

It's so pervasive, so obvious, that it often gets forgotten or pushed into the background. Because it is the underlying motivation for so many of your coworkers, it's easy to forget that it's there. Bringing it to the front of your mind as you work will radically change the way you see the work everyone is doing.

You are not perfect.

But neither is anyone else.

I know what you're expecting: a big thing about how everyone makes mistakes and we need to stay positive and move on and not get hung up on failure and blah, blah, blah.

That's true, but that's not what this is about.

Most people understand deep down that they are not perfect. We see our mistakes. Some people are better at hiding it from themselves. They blame others. They deflect. They can't admit it. But most people understand that perfection isn't even ideal, let alone possible.

Here's the thing, though. Even though we all walk around acting like, "hey, nobody's perfect," we don't *really* go around acting like it.

When was the last time you made a significant mistake at work?

Not one you covered up or didn't affect you. Not a mistake that no one else knew about. A real mistake that you owned up to and it was obvious to everyone that it was your fault?

It tends to not happen.

Why?

Because if you make a small mistake, no one notices except you. Even then, most of the time you don't notice. You just keep rolling. It all comes out in the wash.

If you make a big mistake, an unmistakable mistake, not only do you notice but other people do too. You don't get to make many mistakes like that and keep working at the same job. Maybe one. Sometimes zero. Then you get to start the mistake counter over at zero at another company (if you're lucky).

The byproduct of this system is that you are, in many ways, perfect at work. At least it seems that way to you and to others. But you're not perfect, of course.

The weird thing is that you will likely look at your coworkers like they are *not* perfect because you know deep down that no one is. But the same rules apply to them. They either haven't screwed up big enough to get fired or the screw ups are easy to miss and haven't caught up with them.

The nature of the way we work at many companies is that your screw ups affect someone else. The reason you don't see those screw ups is because your mistakes rarely affect you directly. And when they do, you often don't see them as mistakes.

Imagine that you prepare a report for another department. They plan to use this report to make decisions. You make an error on a single line, a number that's slightly inflated. You don't notice of course because it doesn't affect you.

They don't notice either because the number seems like it could be correct and they have no reason to question it.

This goes on for a while.

Eventually someone notices the error. Maybe they point it out to you. Maybe you fix it for the next report. Train keeps rolling.

Except, they've been using incorrect information to make decisions for who knows how long?

This kind of thing is happening to you and to everyone else you work with all the time. It's not just that everyone makes mistakes. It's that these mistakes are part of the fabric of work, the reality of your job. These imperfections are part of you, them, the organization, and everything you do.

We act like we are perfect when it is convenient for us, which is almost always. We act like others are perfect when it is convenient for us, which is almost never. The times we are critical is when the errors are egregious. But the reality is that errors of various magnitude are happening all around you all the time.

They have a job (and so do you).

"I wouldn't ask them to do something that I wouldn't do myself."

How many times have you heard your boss or someone else at work say that phrase or something like it? How many times have *you said it*?

I'll bet you've heard that a lot.

On the surface, that sounds nice. Noble, even. It makes a leader sound good to say it, especially to a bunch of people she is about to tell to do something. But is it true?

No, of course not.

All day long leaders are asking people to do things that they would not do themselves. Maybe they don't know how to do it. Maybe they literally *can't* do it. Maybe they wouldn't be the best person to do it. Maybe the truth is that the skills the leader brings to the table due to time, talent, practice, and ability, mean that there are simply some things they shouldn't be spending time doing.

Harsh, I know.

You could say, 'Well, the leader is saying they *would* do it, so that counts, right?"

Not really. Maybe they are not physically able to do it. Maybe it is not their area of expertise.

The reality is that the saying is trite and condescending. For example, it's almost always used when the leader is about to ask someone to do something boring, tedious, nasty, painful, tiresome, or repetitive. You know, those things don't mean the same thing to everyone. Oh, and those things are sometimes someone's actual job.

If I ask you to clean the bathroom, and your job is to literally keep the bathroom clean, then that's the job you were hired to do and agreed to do. How is that any different than if I ask you to update the network? Repair the vehicle? Read the contract? Attend the meeting? Or any of the other million things that we do every day to get work done?

It's all important or we wouldn't need to do it. And it's all work or we wouldn't need to *pay for it to get done*!

The next time you are about to say that you wouldn't ask someone to do something you wouldn't do yourself, consider what you are really saying.

I wouldn't go up on my roof to make a repair. Why? I'm genuinely worried that I would hurt myself. I would fall. Instead of making the repair, I would make the situation worse. Would I ask someone else to make the repair (and pay them handsomely to do it)? Hell yes I would.

This happens all the time. It's just less obvious. Most of the people you work with and who work for you are doing things that you have no business doing yourself. You have a job. Do that job. Do the job you are there to do and make no apologies when you expect everyone else to do the same.

Email is the devil.

Email is one of the worst ways to communicate with other people at work. For real!

Some of you may be nodding right now. You may even agree with me. But I'll bet you are still sending emails. It's as if you think the rules don't apply to you.

It's easy to misunderstand each other through email. It's easy to miscommunicate. It's really easy to sound angry, anxious, offensive, defensive, and downright frustrated through email. You'd think after all these years we would give each other a little grace. But no. Instead we fume and rage when we get an email from our coworkers or boss.

Everyone always asks what the one thing I would change if I could go back in time. Don't get me wrong, there are a lot of noble things to change if I had the power. But I'd be willing to bet that getting rid of email would improve things.

Why is email such a problem? Email is fundamentally broken.

Email feels immediate, but it's not. It allows you to bend time around your own wants and needs and thrust it on other people. That means for many of us we walk into a barrage of "work" that's already been done by people who are not on the same schedule. In the past, they would have had to seek us out and communicate. But not anymore. Now, you can just leave a message for someone else to deal with.

What's worse is that when you do get someone on the same schedule as you, email turns into a slow-motion and frustrating conversation. Back and forth. Over and over. It could have been a quick phone call, but instead it's a deranged and distracted exercise in miscommunication.

Do you know what's even crazier with email?

Imagine if you wrote me a letter. But you decided to make ten identical copies of the letter and send them out at the same time to a bunch of people that have nothing to do with the letter. That would be weird, right?

Right?

Well, how come you do it with your emails?

Why are you copying anyone on an email? What possible purpose can that serve? If your email is not TO someone (one particular person), you're doing it wrong. If you are adding more people to the email because you hope some kind of action happens, you're also doing it wrong. If you are adding people to the email because you are trying to cover your bases or get someone in trouble, you are definitely doing something wrong.

Send less emails.

See how that changes your work process. It *will* change it. For the better.

Most emails do not matter.

Respond to less emails.

Write your emails to a particular person. Don't copy other people on your emails. If you need to respond to an email, that probably should have been a phone call. If you need to copy multiple people on your email, that probably should have been a meeting.

Use the right tool for the job. Expect others who you work with to do the same.

If no one is running the meeting, you run the meeting.

Meetings are awful.

We've all been to bad meetings. We've all been to okay meetings. But in general, meetings are just awful. It always feels like there's so much blah, blah, blah. Does anything get done?

Well, yes.

Yes, in reality meetings can and do help move things forward. Sometimes it's getting everyone on the same page. Sometimes it's knowing that there is accountability for a project or process. Sometimes it's a check-in for progress on a strategic initiative. Sometimes it's a way for people to connect and come up with new ideas or better ways to get things done. Whatever it is, meetings have value.

But they are still awful.

What takes a good meeting down quick is when no one seems to be running the meeting.

Be the hero. Run the meeting.

It may not even be your meeting. That doesn't matter. Pull people into the conversation. Reiterate what's been said (but give credit where credit is due)! Stand at the whiteboard or flipchart or keyboard and start documenting key themes as you hear them. Circle back to those themes and ask for more information. Seek consensus.

If you actively engage in the meeting, and use that engagement to bring everyone else along with you, it does at least two important things.

First, it makes the meeting less boring and useless for you. Think of it as a chance to practice your presentation skills, your leadership skills, and your communication skills. Have fun with it. If it's not your meeting, the stakes are usually low. You can get away with a lot. Ask crazy questions. Connect the dots for people. Challenge yourself!

Second, it makes the meeting less boring and useless for everyone else. People love leaders. They need leaders. Everyone will be grateful that you are taking the lead and moving the process forward. It doesn't even matter if you are bad at it. What matters is that *someone* is leading. You'll be surprised how much you can actually get done with someone moving things along.

I'm not suggesting that you start bulldozing every meeting. I'm saying that we often find ourselves in meetings that are meandering and not going anywhere. If there is no clear leadership, step up.

This ends up paying off outside of meetings as well. People will come to know you better and appreciate the way that you get things done. You will start getting invited to meetings with the expectation that you are going to *help* just by being there. I've been to so many meetings that had nothing to do with my department or function, just because everyone knew that we would get things done if I was on the invite list. And I learned a bunch about the organization and myself because of it!

Never miss a chance to learn. Never miss a chance to teach. Never sit through another boring meeting.

Everyone is telling a story.

No one is telling the truth.

The people you work with aren't lying exactly. It's not intentional. It's more that there's only so much time in the day, so you get the version of things that takes the least amount of time to produce the desired effect.

It's an important distinction to master. When you are talking with your colleagues, your boss, or your team, remember that everyone is spinning a story. You fit somewhere in that story.

Have you ever found out what someone thinks about you, maybe even someone you've worked with for a long, long time, and thought, "That's crazy! That's not me at all!" Well, that's because it's *not you*. It's their *story of you*. Of course it's not the real you. It's a combination of the version of you they see in small bursts at work and the story they've written for you.

Those moments of disconnect are happening all around you all the time. You're doing it too. You have stories you've written in your head about each and every person you work with, who they are, how they respond, what they think of things. Most of it is a convenient fiction. It's well-meaning. It even sometimes feels real. But it's not.

If you are reading this now and strongly disagreeing with me, think about what you "know" of me when you read this. Do you know me? No. Of course not. But, you already have a sense of how I might be to work with. Would I be a direct communicator? Arrogant? Thought-provoking? Mean? That's your story.

And stories have a way of taking on a life of their own. Before you meet someone at work, there's a good chance that someone else told *your story* to them. Not your real story, but the one they wrote in their own head about you. Now that new person you've never met before thinks they know something about it and it becomes part of their story about you.

This is startling to see unfold when you are at an after hours work event and someone you work with meets your significant other. "Isn't he so funny?" "It must be tough living with him." "What's it like to live with someone so positive and easygoing?" Stories, stories, stories.

I'm not talking about how we all present different aspects of ourselves at work, home, around family, friends, playing sports, or in any of another million facets of our lives. I'm talking about how there is very little time for someone to know you at work. Most of the time we are, well, working! So the stories take on a life of their own.

The focus here is to be aware that people are telling stories about you, to themselves and to others. And that you are doing the same about them!

That's because you are a superhero.

Over the course of many years, I've coached many employees for performance. Many of you will read the word, "coach," and think of something negative. Get over it. We need more coaches. And we need more people willing to be coached.

When I tell you that I had a basketball coach or a baseball coach, you don't immediately think that I got in trouble or needed to be put on a performance plan. But in business, that's often what people think when they are about to go into a coaching session.

Admit it. That's what you would think.

That's not the case at all. Your baseball coach is trying to help you be the best player the world has ever seen. Or at least the best player you can possibly be. Your business coach is trying to help you see how you fit into the organization, how to leverage your unique skills and abilities to provide maximum value, and ultimately how if you get this right the entire team can win. That's what the coach does. Your role in all of this is to *be coached*. It takes two people to make this work.

In these coaching sessions, the best performers will inevitably fall into a negative place. They will start to complain, usually about the poor performance of others. Sometimes, it's what they think I want to hear. It isn't. But people like to gossip. The complaint usually starts with the phrase, "Why can't they just…."

Why can't they just… do better? Get more done? Stay on top of their own work? Do it right? Stop screwing up?

I've heard it all.

My response is always the same: I slowly and carefully look them straight in the eye and say, "That's because you are a superhero."

Your best performers are essentially superheroes. They are better. More productive. Faster. Easier to work with. Get more done in less time. Don't cause problems. And are constantly fixing problems that everyone else causes. If everyone else is a hero, they are superheroes.

Sometimes when I'm thinking about particular supervisors, I'm pretty sure there's nothing "super" about them. We should just call them "visors," but every once in a while someone lives up to the title. Those are the people who will ask you the "Why can't they just…" question.

If you're reading this book, there is a strong possibility that you are a superhero at work. When you get frustrated at how everyone else performs, remember that you have skills and abilities far beyond those of your colleagues. You have potential. You are going places. Let your coach do what they do best. Engage in the coaching process. Reach your potential. Stop worrying about why everyone else can't get it done.

Repeat yourself.

Repeat yourself.

Many strong leaders are doers and thinkers, catalysts and dynamos, supporters and nurturers, and every other quality in between. One common thing I've noticed though is that no matter what your leadership style is, you tend to move on from things quickly.

Got it. Done. What's next? Yes, I understand. What else do you have for me?

This can come across as impatient. It's something to be aware of when you are working with other people, especially people who may be new to the organization or in entry-level positions. But that's not the biggest problem with this quality. The biggest problem is that just because you've moved on mentally doesn't mean that everyone else has.

In fact, most people aren't even keeping up in the first place.

I've worked with many strong leaders who can read an email once, glance at it really, and come away with the meaning and understand what they need to do next. The same can be said for a quick conversation or a quick review of a contract. These people are drawing upon a wealth of experience to quickly analyze a situation, integrate it with what they know, come up with a plan, execute, and then move on. Great!

Great, except no one has any idea what they are talking about.

It's a trap to assume that everyone is running at your speed. They aren't. If they were, they probably wouldn't need you to do whatever it is you were hired to do. This seems obvious if you take a moment to think about it. Yet, in the pressure of the moment, even the best leaders will not check for understanding. It seems basic enough, so the thought of checking in with the people you are leading doesn't even occur to you. But it should.

What's an even bigger trap is to move on without repeating yourself. Assume that most people aren't hearing you. They are distracted. They have other concerns. Sometimes they simply aren't ready to hear what you are saying at that moment. You need to repeat yourself.

The frustrating part of this for leaders is that you have a finite amount of time to communicate, and so many important things to say. So, you say a lot. And most of it whizzes by the people who most need to really hear you.

The pressure is on you to figure out the most important parts of your message, say them once, then say them again. And again. And again. Find new ways to say the same thing. Find new ways to communicate the same thing. But always, always repeat yourself.

Be clear and concise.

Give every person your absolute peak performance, but...

Don't waste time on morons.

You probably think you can multitask, but you can't. No, really. It's time someone told you the truth. You can do a bad job at multiple things. I believe that. But you can't do a world class job at multiple things at the same time.

Be world class.

If you are in a meeting, *be in that meeting*. If you are on a phone call, *be on that phone call*. If you are writing an email, *focus on that email*.

This sounds like obvious stuff. It's what you would want from the people around you. But do you focus on what you are doing? Probably not. If you're like almost everyone, you "multitask." And you are awful at it.

Some people will even make a backhanded apology before a meeting by saying, "Sorry, I'm going to be multitasking during this meeting, but I'm listening." No you aren't. When people do that to me, I stop talking. You'd be surprised how long you can sit there in silence before the multitasker notices that something is missing.

Your time is precious. Throw yourself into your work. By all means, do the stuff that matters. But you will be a million times more effective when you admit to yourself that multitasking is utter nonsense *and start acting like it.*

When you switch to focusing on one thing at a time, you'll start to notice that some people are a massive waste of your time. Sometimes it's because they are trying to multitask while you are committed to accomplishing something. Sometimes it's because you'll see with clarity what's actually going on when you take the time to focus. Either way, you can magnify your effectiveness considerably by not wasting time on these people.

Give them a chance, first, though. Try something like, "This project is important to me and to the success of the company. For the duration of this meeting, I am committing to turning off my email and putting my phone on do not disturb. Can I expect the same from you?"

Sometimes, you just need to be the person who goes first.

This comes up often when coaching an employee. They are busy. They aren't getting something important done. I ask them if they are blocking out time to work on it, time where the phone is off, email is off, the door is shut, and they aren't getting messages. They always tell me no, like I don't understand, like there is no way that they could possibly do that. They explain how important they are, how people are always calling them, stopping by their office, asking questions. It's mission critical stuff!

Then I remind them that we've been in a meeting for the past hour and the world is still turning.

They haven't been answering the phone. They haven't checked email. They haven't been at the office for anyone to stop by.

Then I ask them to imagine that instead of meeting with me, they were working on the important project that entire time. How much of it could they have gotten done if they simply focused?

If you want to really drive it home, schedule a meeting with your employee and then cancel at the last minute. Call it a gift. Nah, don't do that. That makes you sound like a jerk. But...

You're supposed to be busy.

You might be working with a manager who is always *swamped*. Same story, different day. How much overtime are they working? How much overtime is the team putting in to get everything done?

None.

Oh, so you aren't busy?

Then they switch tactics and tell you that they were so clever they figured out a way to magically get everything done during the 40 hours they work during the week. Everyone on the team did too.

Ah, yes. Magic. Strange how that works out. Have you ever noticed that when someone has 40 hours to get everything done it takes 40 hours to do it?

Have you ever had a manager come to you and suggest that they reduce headcount or hours? Maybe if there's an incentive in it for them. Maybe. Most of the time you just hear about how busy everyone is.

When did everyone get the impression that you aren't supposed to be busy? Of course you're supposed to be busy! You were hired to do work that needed to be done. That's what work is. If it wasn't that, we would call it something else.

This all needs to be within reason. I'm sure some people are more busy than others. I'm sure some people have busy times and less busy times. But in general, you *are* supposed to "feel busy" at work.

When I feel busy at work, I think, "Oh good. I'm busy. My job matters. I'm contributing. This is a good feeling." That needs to be the mindset. When an employee tells me that they are busy, I'm always interested to know what they are working on. If it's the right thing, and if they are actually busy, that's great! That's what we are all here to do!

Each person can only do what they can do. Depending on the job, that may be the work right in front of you like making a sandwich or answering a phone call. For other jobs, it may be working through a multi-part project to hit a future delivery date. Whatever it is, your job as the manager is to manage to the desired outcome. But your job as an employee is to be busy (with the work that matters).

This isn't rocket surgery.

Is it hard to breathe up there on your high horse? Did you hurt your shoulder patting yourself on the back?

Here's the tough truth: Your job isn't nearly as difficult as you think it is.

When you hear about someone else's job, do you immediately think that it sounds difficult? Like you couldn't do it? No. It sounds like a lot of words and pomp and circumstance.

That's how you sound to everyone else.

Schools are pushing out people all day long who can do your job at least as well as you can. Probably better.

More often than not, the thing that keeps you in your job is not that you are great at it. It's momentum. You're doing a good enough job that there's no reason to look for someone else. You're there. You show up. You mostly get things done. You mostly don't cause trouble.

Stop making it so complicated.

Some of you may read this and find it freeing. I see employees who put tons of pressure on themselves. Action with no results. The pressure isn't coming from anywhere. Their boss just wants them to show up and do the work that's in front of them. There's a lot of kicking and screaming and making this complicated when none of that matters.

It's like switching banks. People don't switch banks because they heard there was better service at the bank down the street. They switch banks when the bank they are at screws up so profoundly that they can't possibly stand banking there one more day. And then they wait a couple of months before they actually switch banks anyway!

In the same way, your boss doesn't fire you because you're doing an okay job. You get fired when you profoundly screw up, and usually months after you should have been fired!

The point is, take some time to figure out if your job is difficult because you're making it something it isn't supposed to be. I'm willing to bet that *you* bring a lot of what makes it difficult to the table. Stop telling everyone how difficult it is. Drop the act.

We're not building rockets.

Unless you are.

A vanishingly small number of people reading this are actually building rockets. For the rest of you, calm down.

I appreciate people taking things seriously. No matter what you do for work, it's serious. Even writing a sitcom is serious business. There are deadlines. Jobs are on the line. People are depending on you to come through. I get it.

Sometimes people are overwhelmed with things that simply don't matter. Good leaders help people focus on what truly matters in a situation. Often that means pointing out things people are worried about that don't impact what they are working on. You only think you are building rockets. But you aren't.

It's a delicate balance. You want people to be dedicated and take their jobs seriously. But it is common that people start deciding for themselves what is important at work. I see it all the time. Suddenly something you couldn't care less about is, for them, like building a rocket. It's that serious. Everything depends on it.

Imagine if you *were* building rockets. Suddenly you have a clear goal: get this rocket safely launched by a certain date. Wouldn't that be nice? Most of us lack obvious goals. For most work situations, the goal might be something more difficult to pin down or with multiple acceptable outcomes. When the goal isn't clear, people come up with their own goals. Tangible goals feel more comfortable. So, every little thing your employees have decided is important is on the same level for them as building a rocket.

It's like spraying for spiders.

Most of the people I know don't like spiders. And if they do like spiders, they don't like surprise spiders crawling across the floor. Surprise spiders are the worst. Depending on where you live, there might be a time during the year where you "get spiders." They just start showing up. They are suddenly just *there*. You start seeing them a couple of times per day. You start wondering about how many *other spiders* are already in the house that you can't see.

What do you do?

You call up an exterminator to spray for spiders. They wander around the house, spraying whatever it is that they spray. They spray along the outside of the house and around the windows. They spray the vents. They check around. You're good to go.

Inevitably, you see another spider in the house. So, you call the exterminator. What gives? There's a spider in here.

And the exterminator says, "Imagine how many there would be if we *didn't spray for spiders*?"

Then they sell you a monthly spider spraying service.

This type of thing happens all the time at work. People do things that are like spraying for spiders. *You* do things that are like spraying for spiders. Then when the spiders do show up, everyone says, "Imagine if we didn't spray for spiders, though."

People all around you are going through their workdays updating reports, reviewing newsletters and data, keeping up on the news, evaluating internal memos, watching pre-recorded seminars, and generally "spraying for spiders." The worry is that any one of those million things could be a spider and no one likes spider surprises.

It's like being worried that every time you reach for a towel or turnover a teacup there's going to be a spider lurking. Instead we get caught up at work looking at every piece of irrelevant information because there could be something important lurking. The one time you got caught flat footed in a meeting because you missed an important email sticks in your mind. Suddenly, every email is the one that could come back to bite you. The one time your boss asked for a report and you didn't have it updated sticks in your mind. Suddenly, every report matters.

I'm not saying there aren't important things for you to focus on at work. I'm saying the opposite: there *are* important things for you to focus on at work. Everything can't be the most important thing. You can't treat everything like it has a spider inside of it.

Be honest with yourself and take an accounting of everything you worked on today (or better yet for the week). How much of it actually mattered? How much of it was made up of things that you do because it is part of a routine that was laid down a long time ago based on one off incidents that you *never want to have happen again*?

You were surprised by the spider in the shower that one time. By god, it's never going to happen to you again.

Your job is to decide who you are not going to make happy.

Okay, okay, you can take the positive position on this one and reword it as, "Your job is to decide who you *are* going to make happy," but the point is the same: you aren't going to make everyone happy.

We've all heard before that you can't make everyone happy. In general, people accept this and understand it. Let's take it a step further, though. If you assume that no matter what you do you aren't going to make everyone happy, then what we are really saying is that you need to *decide* who you aren't going to make happy. This isn't something you leave up to chance. Your job is to weigh all the options and literally figure out who you aren't going to make happy.

When you realize that it's your decision *and your job* to decide who you aren't going to make happy, everything changes. Look, I'm not saying you shouldn't consider ways to make the most people happy. That could be good business if you can figure out a way to do it. I'm not saying there won't be a rare time when everything just works out. But those are the exceptions. The reality is that day-in and day-out, you are going to make decisions that don't fall evenly on everyone affected by those decisions.

You aren't just leaving it up to chance. You are deciding who won't like the outcome. This gives you the opportunity to communicate with those people who are affected by your decision. Sometimes talking through your options helps everyone get on board, even if they aren't benefiting from what you decided. Sometimes you'll find that you were wrong about how your decision is affecting certain people. But if you think about it as a decision, you have more options about how to communicate the outcome.

One thing in the morning. One thing in the afternoon.

This is going to sound crazy, unbelievable even. Hear me out. If you get one important thing done every morning and one important thing done every afternoon, day in and day out, you will be the most effective employee your company has ever seen. Ever.

Don't get me wrong, most people are doing things all day long. You are, too. You're making phone calls, typing stuff up, sending emails, attending meetings, sending reports, drawing up plans, and whatever else gets you through the day. Most of that stuff isn't *important*. It might be necessary, but it doesn't move things forward; it keeps things from moving backward.

Important stuff moves things forward.

Think about your last workday. What *important* thing did you do in the morning? What was something you did that was significant in even a small way to move the organization forward? It could be anything. Can you think of something concrete that you could tell me about in a 30 second elevator ride?

How about in the afternoon? Same deal. I'm sure you did a lot of stuff. It might have even felt necessary at the time. But looking back now, what do you have to talk to me about in a 30 second elevator ride that moved the business forward?

You might be thinking that everything you did was what needed to be done. I might agree with you. We all have a lot to do every day to keep the business running, to keep it from going backward. But moving the business forward is something different. It is something new. You'll know it when it happens because you'll need to *make it happen*. It's something you can describe to someone else that doesn't sound like more of the same.

Imagine if you did this every day, twice a day. Every day, you did something that you could talk about in a 30 second elevator ride that moved the needle. Are you getting the picture? No one could keep up with you.

You would be a superstar.

It's alarmingly simple to be a superstar at your company. Most people get through the work day by keeping the business from moving backward. Occasionally, they may even move the business forward. But if moving the business forward is your daily habit? Buckle up.

Do what you can do.

So simple. And yet, this is one of the most destructive behaviors I see at work. What I see is people sitting around stuck on a problem and unable to move forward. They have a million other things they could be doing, but nope. They have eyes for only the problem in front of them.

This is seldom obvious to the person involved. It's subtle. It's happened to you. Your mind keeps returning to the one thing that you can't do, oblivious to the myriad other things you could be doing. Time starts slipping away. You're getting behind. But you're so focused on this one thing you can't do that everything else starts to become a problem. You miss deadlines. Your work gets sloppy. You stop being responsive. Pretty soon, the problem is solved. Not because you solved it, but because it's not your problem anymore since you no longer work at the company.

This happens to smart people, too. The more inwardly focused you are, the easier it is to fall victim to this mindset. The reminder is to simply *do what you can do*. There are oodles of more things you can do during the workday than the things you can't do. The worst thing is to be the person that just waits for someone else to come along and solve the problem.

The trap is that when you hit a roadblock if you keep putting it off, that's not a solution either. It will come back to bite you if you avoid getting something done. This isn't about avoidance. This is about understanding when you can't do something, but then not letting it stop you from doing everything else.

Too many times I've seen people who are confident that they can get everything else done spend hours and days on something they should have set aside or asked for help to accomplish only to find that they didn't get anything done. A small problem then turns into a big problem. And big problems get resolved one way or the other.

During your workday, you will have a million things happen. Phone calls, emails, meetings, files, reports, and whatever else your business needs to get done. Inevitably, there will be that one thing that comes along that you've never seen before. It's intriguing. You get pulled into it. You start to ask around. You start researching. You're down the rabbit hole on some forum post from five years ago. Something that should have taken a few minutes has now taken up the better part of a day. And everything else that you could have handled easily is now behind. Sound familiar?

The weird part is that managers will often reward this behavior by applauding the tenacity of the employee who stuck with a problem until they solved it. They will gloss over the fact that a bunch of other stuff didn't get done or had to be shuffled off to the other employees who now have to hear about what a great job you did sticking with the problem. Nine times out of ten, that's not how the problem actually gets solved, but we remember the one time it worked out.

Start setting boundaries when you run across something new. You have no idea how long it will take to resolve whatever it is. By definition, it's unknown. Have a strategy for approaching those situations that allows you to continue to do what you can do.

The difference between 0 and 1 is infinity.

The difference between 1 and 2 is 1.

It seems that human nature is set up for people to not notice how this works. People will take on more and more tasks without understanding the consequences. It usually happens a little at a time. The root cause is surprising. It's laziness. Let me explain.

How can doing *more* things be *lazy*?

It's a combination of a few factors.

It's difficult to stone-cold say "no." Suddenly, you have a new task. You tell yourself it's just a little thing, takes a few minutes, no big deal. That's one. It happens over and over and now you are spending more and more of your day doing just one more thing.

Another way this happens is that something needs to be done, so you do it. You don't do it right, but you just need to move on so you get it done. Then it happens again. What you did before worked, so you do it again. Boom. Now *doing it wrong* is your process.

Both of these things are lazy. You either shouldn't be doing it at all. Or if you are going to do it, you should be doing it right.

This is happening all day, every day. Everyone you work with is being sent messages, emails, and reports. There are phone calls and meetings. At every turn someone is being presented with the opportunity to start doing something they haven't done before. This even happens at the strategic level. Your business is constantly being presented with an opportunity to do something new. Most of the time, you won't even know about it. A customer asks one of your sales team to whip up a new report. They do. Now you're in the report business. Next you're in the data analysis business. Repeat. Your employees are doing things all day long that you aren't paying them to do. The worst part? They feel overwhelmed with all of this "work" you never asked them to do!

They made it all up!

And it's so easy. You don't even see it coming.

There are countless things your employees aren't doing today. The amount of things they are doing is infinitesimally small compared to what they *could* be doing. Starting something new requires systems, process, procedures, training, coordination, strategy, timing, and execution. Yet, here they are starting new stuff all the time!

So what happens is customer X asks your sales team for a new report. The sales team creates the report. You just went from 0 to 1. Something new you weren't doing before now exists. You made the jump from nothing to something, 0 to 1. Suddenly, it doesn't seem like such a big deal to create the same report for customer Y. Do you see where this is going? Your sales team is already working on this report, so adding one more report for one more customer isn't a big deal. Right?

Wrong.

This is how productivity and time gets squandered. Once the motorcycle has jumped across the gap from 0 to 1, it's a short ride from 1 to 2, 2 to 3, and so on. The worst part of this is how it gets stuck somewhere short of actually being useful. It's been put together by people who do not understand the impact, in a way that is inefficient and haphazard, and creates stress and anxiety for the employee. Once the new manager joins the team, the change is now permanent. The new manager will be afraid to "undo" anything that's "working." After a few team members rotate out, no one will ever again question how they went from 0 to 1.

Your job is to stop 0 from turning into 1 in almost every situation. And if it is going to turn into 1, make sure there is a plan to get from 1 to something useful. Build it from the ground up with a goal in mind, not just to get something off your plate.

Whether you are new to managing a team or you've been managing the same team for a while, your day is likely full of items that went from 0 to 1 at some point in the past. It's time to make some tough choices. Sometimes you need to stop doing something that isn't making an impact. Doing less of a stupid thing is still stupid. Stop doing the stupid thing altogether.

The knife cuts both ways.

It cuts going in and it cuts coming out.

This lesson comes up a lot. In big ways and in small ways, we often find ourselves in a situation where we need to make a tough decision. This is a reminder that when we are finally ready to make that tough decision, it doesn't only affect one person or group.

Over and over when I'm coaching people about making tough decisions, the person tends to focus on only one side of the equation. The conversation either revolves around how difficult it is going to be for *them* or how difficult it will be for the *other person.* That's all well and good, but the reality is that the decision is tough for everyone involved. If it was easy it would already be done.

Whether it's canceling a contract, discontinuing a product, telling someone that even though they are doing their best it isn't good enough, or moving on to a new team or leadership role, it can become too easy to focus on one side of the equation. I find that the side you focus on tends to suggest a lot about who you are as a person. I'll leave that there for you to pick up.

The problem is that there's no way to leave the knife in. That's only half of a decision. If you continue to consider only one side of the equation, you end up with a lot of knives sticking out of a lot of people. Or a lot of knives sticking out of yourself. It catches up with you one way or the other.

If you want to outrun the devil, start by tying your shoes.

I could just as easily say, "First Things First," but that doesn't quite capture this one. So many times I work with people who are trying to do everything. It gets overwhelming. They've built a house of cards that's teetering, waiting for a small gust of wind to come along and turn it all into a jumbled pile.

You've seen this before: Executives who are barely holding it together day after day, burning the midnight oil to stay on top of deadlines, throwing work/life balance to the wind in hopes of getting through one more day. These people are lying to themselves. It's like trying to "catch up" on sleep when you pull an all-nighter. Maybe if it happens once in a while, you'll be okay. You drink some coffee and power through. Maybe. But when it happens every single day, the devil *will* catch up with you.

The good news is that even if you are in the middle of this, going back to the basics will dig you out. Your shoes are untied. You need to tie them.

Remember the last time you told yourself you would slip on some shoes to go get the mail? You didn't bother tying your shoes because you weren't going to be doing any running and it really didn't matter. So you loped out to the mailbox with your shoes untied. Maybe you tripped on a loose lace, but you were sauntering along so no big deal. No harm, no foul.

Imagine if you did the same thing before the big race? Imagine if you didn't bother to tie your shoes because you showed up late to the race where everyone was counting on you to do your best. Well hey, you showed up, right? That should count for something. Besides, you were busy with a thousand other things, so you didn't tie your shoes. How would that turn out? Not great.

Yet, that's what I see happen every day. People showing up to work without having done the basic things to prepare for the race. When the devil does show up, they aren't ready to run. And make no mistake: the devil shows up. In force. Ready to race. And his shoes? Tied up nice and tight. He even stretched out before the big day.

It could be someone calling in sick before a big meeting. It could be an information security breach. It could be a lost file, a missed phone call, coffee spilled on your best shirt in the middle of a work day. Whatever it is, it will happen. And when it does, you won't be ready because you didn't do the basics.

And here's the kicker: it happens every day. The devil shows up in little ways, all day every day. The little miscommunications. The missed opportunities. You're out there running around with your shoes untied wondering why you just can't seem to get out from under the avalanche of stuff that gets thrown at you. It's the little trip ups here and there that starts the pile growing.

Take 5 minutes at the end of every work day to write down the simple things you could have done to make your day easier. What's the equivalent to tying your shoes that you've been skipping because you think something else is more important? In the morning, flip open your note from the day before and *tie your shoes before you start working*.

The first thing that you should check when you start your work day is if your shoes are tied. If they aren't, tie them now *before* you start running.

Your glasses are always in the last place you look…

…because once you find them, you stop looking.

On the surface, this seems like a simple statement. Of course you stop looking, you've found your glasses. But we do this all the time at work. We think we've found what we're looking for so we stop looking. We grab for whatever the solution is that is within reach, slap it on the problem, and move on.

We've all been in situations where it feels like we are putting out fires all day. Our glasses are missing and as soon as we find them, we stop looking. There's a fire over there! Put it out. Onto the next fire. Put that one out. Oh look, another fire. We spend all day fighting fires often by using the first thing that looks like a solution.

If you take a step back, we all know that the real problem is what caused the fires in the first place. It's great that you found your glasses and stopped looking, but that's not the problem. The problem is why you lost your glasses in the first place.

There will always be problems. Things will not go according to plan. The challenge is to realize that providing a solution to that specific problem is like finding your glasses and moving on. It's a solution, but it's not the right one. The real solution is to figure out why you lost your glasses to begin with and put a solution in place to avoid that problem in the future.

Changing the way you work to refocus on solving the problem not only once, but forever, takes discipline. It means that when you think you've found a solution to the problem at hand, your next step should always be to figure out what caused the problem and solve that. That's the real problem.

Stop losing your glasses.

New Line Dancers Go to the Middle

During the course of your career, you will sometimes be the new person. New to a job, new to a company, new to a position, or new to a team. You will also sometimes be managing a new person or adding a new person to your team. No matter the situation, there are a couple of ways to start.

Line dancing can be tricky. If you aren't familiar with the moves, it can be extremely difficult to figure out what you are supposed to be doing. There's one strange quality of line dancing, which is why I like to use it as an example for bringing new people onto a team: Line dancing involves turning around.

Imagine that you are learning a new line dance. The dance hall is full of people who all know the dance. Some people are comfortable. Most people are doing a passable job and executing the dance. Then there's you. You've done some line dancing before, but you don't know this particular dance. So, you watch for a while. Maybe you pick up the pattern or a few moves while you are standing on the sidelines. Finally, you get up the courage to wander to the edge of the dance floor and join in. You start dancing and things seem to be going fine. Sure, you're awkward and miss a few moves here and then and then it happens. The dancers turn so that you can't see them anymore. You're lost, trying to look over your shoulder to know what to do next. It's a mess. You move off the floor thinking that you need some more time to observe and practice. Your confidence is shot. You don't even bother getting back out there to try again.

What's wrong here?

You don't want to be embarrassed. You don't want to throw off the rest of the dancers. You have the confidence to give it a try. And then it all falls apart. The problem is that when the dancers turn, you can no longer see them. What's the solution? Walk to the middle of the floor before you start dancing. When the dancers turn, you will always have another dancer to look at in front of you. This makes a world of difference to the outcome.

The lesson here is that if you are new or you are onboarding someone new, it is almost always right to put them in the busiest situation with the most people around them for support. There will be exceptions to this, of course. Sometimes jobs are dangerous to the new employee or the outcome of failure can be dangerous to the customer. But in general, if you can choose to put yourself in a situation with the most opportunities for experience, you will almost always be in the situation with the most incidental support.

For example, take an employee who is being hired to work in a call center. The manager has two choices of where to place that employee. Do they put the employee on the shift with the least amount of calls so that they can move at a slower pace? Or do they put that employee on the shift with the most calls? Our inclination is often to give the new employee time to develop by putting them on the shift with less calls. This is almost always wrong. Putting the employee in the busier situation creates more opportunities for experience and usually means that the employee has more opportunities for support. In a matter of weeks, the new employee will have more experience than an employee who has been on the slower shift for months.

Do the last thing you want to do.

It's easy to figure out what to do next. It's always the last thing you want to do.

Every single person falls somewhere on the procrastination continuum. Most of us know where we are on that line. Sometimes we procrastinate with projects at home, but are proactive at work. Sometimes it's the opposite. Sometimes we are proactive with friends and family, but push off caring for ourselves. Whatever the case may be for you personally, this is about you at work.

Many of us have a certain amount of autonomy over our time at work. This is more true in some positions than in others, of course. What matters here is that everyone already knows what they are supposed to do. It's the thing they are not doing. Because, and focus here, if they were doing that thing, then that thing would be done, and it wouldn't be the thing they are avoiding.

That probably doesn't make much sense on the first read through. This is one of those scenarios that once you see it, you won't be able to unsee it. We need to get you there if you're not there already.

I believe in coaching employees for performance. I've spent countless hours in coaching sessions listening to employees talk to me about what they need to do to be successful. They already have the answers. You can usually get them there just by asking. The common question is, "What are you working on right now?" But that question is not the important one. The important question is, "What *should* you be working on right now?"

This question opens up a world of possibilities.

I'm asking you that question right now. Think about yourself at work. What should you be working on right now? My guess is that what you should be working on and what you are actually working on is not 100% congruent. You know that there are things you should be doing, but aren't. You are avoiding those things. And almost always, those things you are avoiding are the things that matter the most.

We find ways to busy ourselves with things that give us reason or justification for not doing the things we are avoiding. Sometimes we convince ourselves that they are important or just important enough to rationalize not getting those other important things done. It's in our nature. But if you can see the pattern, you can do something about it. Push yourself directly at the thing you are avoiding.

This can be anything from a difficult project or conversation to a tedious but necessary task. Whatever it is, getting it done will set you apart from everyone else. As they continue to avoid the difficult work, you'll be crossing things off your list.

Have a plan, work a plan.

We've all worked with people who do not seem to spend any time thinking about what they are about to do. They have been successful in school or with previous bosses or teams, so they keep on doing whatever seems like the next best thing. The result in almost all cases is a house-of-cards because there is no predictable system for how one thing gets added to another.

I've said to the teams I work with many times that I don't care if they use *my* plan, but they had better use *a* plan. When you challenge someone to plan out what they are doing, it often helps them immediately see where potential problems can arise. It also invites conversations about how to improve on the plan.

When I say the word "plan," many of you are probably thinking about big projects with multiple participants where it is obvious you would want a plan to keep everyone moving in the same direction. While that is an obvious place for a plan, I'm sure that most of us can think of a situation where even though the consequences of failure were significant, there was no plan. So yes, I'm talking about the obvious situations where there should be a plan. But I'm also talking about less obvious situations.

Do you have a plan for working through your email? Many people do not. They do a little of this and a little of that, but there is no clear plan for how to approach something that affects your entire work day, every day. I'm not saying email is your job. I'm saying that for many of us, email is a key way that we communicate with each other. Not having a plan for how you approach your email is ridiculous. If you can't explain to another individual exactly how you work through your email, you don't have a plan.

But simply having a plan is not enough. You have to *work the plan*. Many people spend time coming up with elaborate plans, but never reconcile those plans with what they actually do. What you actually spend your time doing is your plan, so it should match up with what you planned in the first place!

As you go through your work day, every part of it should be planned. Even creative time should be worked into your plan to ensure that it doesn't get crowded out by all of the other competing priorities. It's easy to fall into a pattern of running from one fire to the next. Having a plan and working a plan ensure that your priorities get done.

Every incentive program is also a disincentive program.

People already have an implicit incentive program: do your job and we'll pay you for as long as we need you to keep doing that job. We don't talk about jobs this way, but at a very high level, that's what they are.

Think of it like this, I only have employees because I am unwilling or unable to do all of the profitable work that needs to be done. If there is no profitable work to do, the job will not exist. If I am able to do all of the work, the job should not exist so long as I am also willing to do the work. In other words, I often talk to employees who act as if the job exists *for them* instead of the other way around.

This manifests itself in a lot of strange ways. Employees feel entitled or complain about changes to the job or workload. How many times have you had to redo work because of a mistake or because something outside of your control ruined the work that was already done? So what? Your job is to produce a certain outcome given a certain set of constraints.

Sometimes employees will look at the work produced by other members of the team and then shift their own work down accordingly. People get away with the least amount of effort. This is logically inconsistent, but they evaluate their own work against the closest available benchmark and adjust to it.

To fix this problem, managers will often introduce an incentive program. I want to be clear that I am not talking about jobs that are driven primarily by incentive programs. Sales jobs, for example, are often set up so that the incentive program is the largest part of the compensation. That's fine. Everyone understands that going in. The problem is when we try to use incentive programs on jobs that traditionally do not have separate incentives. This introduces the idea to the employees that everything they do all day long is transactional on an individual basis rather than in the aggregate.

Imagine it like this: You have a spouse. You've been married for a while. You make a deal with your spouse that whoever makes dinner will have to pay the other person the same amount they would have paid to go out to dinner at a restaurant. On the surface, that sounds reasonable. I mean, you would have paid the restaurant to make the dinner, so why not keep it in the family by paying your spouse? The reason is that this turns a natural part of your relationship into something transactional *and pins it to a specific dollar amount.* Substitute "making dinner" for something more intimate and you can see where this might end up.

If you are managing a team of employees that do not typically operate with an incentive program but then decide to introduce an incentive program, you might get better performance for the activities where you have added an incentive. But you will certainly get worse performance for the things where you did *not* add an incentive. You will have simultaneously created a disincentive program for everything that is not explicitly on your new incentive program.

Sometimes this can happen even when you least expect it. Imagine being at a team meeting and recognizing one of your employees for something they did particularly well that week. Sure, you gave them some recognition and that can be good for morale, but what else did you do? You specifically did *not* recognize everyone else. You've implicitly told everyone else that you think this one thing is important enough to get recognition and therefore all the other things are somehow less important. Will they all put two and two together and up with four? Maybe. But you *are* sending a message to everyone about what you value (and don't value) as sure as you are standing there.

There are a lot of lists you do not want to be on.

Make sure that you are not on them.

Where you work, there are tons of departments that are tracking things. Reports being filed. Timecards being stamped and signed. Everything from strategies being set to projects being tracked to training being completed are things that someone somewhere is expecting from you. And when you don't do the things you are supposed to do, you end up on a "list."

I work with a lot of managers. When I see them end up on lists like this, it belies one of two things: 1) a disrespect of the work process or 2) an inability to complete the work process. In other words, you have a job to do. Part of that job is to get certain things done a certain way and by a certain time. If you don't, we need to consider what happened. Either you *can't* do it or you *won't* do it. Which is it?

The feedback I often get at this point is that the manager doesn't consider all of those things to be important or not a priority. This is a golden opportunity to clarify that getting these things done is as much a part of the job as anything else, possibly more so given that only the manager can do these things. You are simply causing grief for another employee somewhere because in your hubris you discount the thing that they think is important.

The other possibility is that the manager is unable to actually get everything done. They do not have the work processes, training, or wherewithal to accomplish the basic tasks of the job that keeps them off lists like this. Almost no one will admit to this. This puts them in a precarious spot. They either knew what they were supposed to do and decided not to, or they knew what they were supposed to do and didn't do it anyway. Neither outcome is good.

Spend the time in your own job to understand what you are supposed to do. Then, make sure that your work processes are aligned with those expectations. You should not be on anyone's list. It is usually the easiest part of your job. It's possibly the most boring part of your job, but necessary nevertheless.

Feel free to start pushing back on processes you think are inefficient or time-wasters *after you've consistently accomplished the things you are supposed to do.* When you are showing up on lists is not the time to push back to your boss that you think those things are stupid or a waste of time. By then, it's too late. You've already demonstrated that you either don't care enough to do your job or you simply can't do your job.

You are not a bad person. You just need more practice.

Stuff will come up in your work life every day that suggests you are a bad person. You'll miss stuff. People will complain about you. You'll feel bad about the things you said and did, the things you meant to do but didn't deliver. If you start thinking about who you let down today, how many times you fell short, and then start thinking about all the things *you didn't even notice* that you did wrong, there's plenty of evidence that you are a bad person.

Unless you are intentionally out there to hurt people, you're not a bad person. You just need more practice. Being a good person is like learning to play an instrument: it takes practice. I understand that this sounds weird, but this principle is about recognizing that you are not naturally going to be good at everything you do. Just like you wouldn't expect to pick up a guitar for the first time and start shredding, why would you think that you can get promoted to being a manager and be great at it? It takes work. Practice. Time. Effort.

Responding thoughtfully to email takes practice. Being great at participating in a meeting takes practice. Knowing when to speak up takes practice. You need to approach your work with an attitude of practice, no different than learning to play the guitar. And just like you couldn't sit there and practice the guitar for eight hours per day and expect to rapidly improve, you won't get opportunities to practice everything at your job all day every day.

I don't know how many coaching sessions I've been in where the employee sitting across from me thinks they are ready for a promotion, but when I ask them to tell me about examples where they demonstrated some important aspect of the job, they can't give me anything except one time they tried and didn't quite pull it off. The best example they have is a time they tried and failed. We can all imagine that if we are given opportunities, of course we would rise to the occasion. How often is that true? It takes practice.

Don't be right, do right.

Some of you are perfectionists. You're bad at it, but you try. It's important to remember that there is no way to *be* right 100% of the time. If you have that expectation for yourself, you will let yourself down. And it isn't reasonable to expect the people you work with to be 100% right all the time. They will make mistakes. They will screw up, sometimes beyond belief.

What you can expect from yourself is that you *do* right 100% of the time. Doing right means that you are making the best decision with the limited information you have. Doing right means that you own up to mistakes instead of covering them up or blaming someone else. We all have multiple opportunities to do right every day. It's a habit. It's as simple as picking up a small piece of trash in the hallway at work instead of stepping over it, not because anyone is watching but because it's the right thing to do.

This principle is asking a lot from you. Many people focus on *being* right, having the right answer, arguing even when deep down they know they are wrong. You cannot be right 100% of the time. If you think you can be right 100% of the time, you are either delusional or dishonest. But you can *do the right thing*. When you switch your mindset, you'll find that your interactions with your job and your coworkers make a lot more sense.

How many times have you talked to someone at work and it's clear to you that they screwed up, but they are arguing with you about why they did what they did. They want to be right even though they are wrong. Does this work on you?

Are you convinced? If they just admit to the mistake and work to make it right, isn't that what you want from them? Guess what? The same applies to you.

No one is out to get you.

Your life is not a movie. You do not work with a bunch of elite ladder-climbers. For the small handful of people who would step on anyone to get ahead, everyone knows what they are about. No one likes them.

It's tempting to think that your coworkers have a personal agenda to get you fired or to make you look bad. And maybe, from time-to-time, if the opportunity presents itself, someone might step through the wide open door. But there is no master plan to get you fired.

Do *you* engineer situations to get your coworkers fired? Do *you* come to work with complicated plans to make your coworkers look bad? Of course not. You come to work to do your job, just like everyone else. If you think someone is out to get you, chances are you are giving them too much credit.

Never ascribe to malice what you can ascribe to stupidity.

I can't count the number of times I've had an employee I'm working with blame something on someone else, accusing that person of doing it on purpose to make them look bad. They genuinely think these people are out to sabotage a project or make them miss an important deadline. And when we talk through what that person would have actually had to do to pull off that masterful piece of deceit it becomes clear that of course they aren't capable of doing that. Even if they wanted to sabotage your project and get you fired, most people are simply incapable of executing a plan like that. If they were that effective at execution, they wouldn't need to sabotage you!

Frankly, you're not so good at what you do that anyone has to go out of their way to get you fired. And if you are that good, they couldn't get you fired anyway. The same way you can tell if someone is up to something at work, your coworkers and boss can tell too.

What happens behind the counter stays behind the counter.

Every job has something equivalent to "the counter." It could be a service desk or a computer screen or a literal counter, but conceptually there are always things that happen "behind the scenes" at every business. This is true even for things that happen between departments or individual members of a team.

This isn't about being opaque. This principle is about acknowledging that no one cares *why* something isn't working or all the things you have to do to make it work. They just want what they want with the least amount of your nonsense along the way. How many times have you been waiting for your order and heard the person behind the counter make an excuse like, "The computer is really slow today." Who cares? What good can come of saying that to the customer? Remember, the "customer" has no idea what it is supposed to look like. The computer could literally be on fire behind the counter, but if the service person acts like this is all perfectly normal, no one would be the wiser.

For those of you who work directly with customers, it is vital that the elements of your job that are frustrating do not come across to the customer. They have no idea that you need to use six different systems to pull up the order and they don't care. They shouldn't have to care. They shouldn't have to carry the burden of your complaints or problems. Those are *your* problems, so keep them to yourself.

The same is true for those of you who work with other departments or with internal customers. Everyone is trying to accomplish their own goals. Spouting off nonsense about how your systems work is not helping anyone. Codes, jargon, slang, systems, requirements, and complications should not enter into the conversation. How many times have you gone to another department to get something done and they tell you they are "short-staffed," or, "down a person." Do you care? No, you just want what you want without the big story. Guess what? They are thinking the same thing *when they come to talk to you*.

Make it look easy.

It's not easy, but your goal should be to make it look easy.

There's nothing worse than someone who looks like they are barely getting by at work, always buried, always putting out fires, always a few minutes late, running from meeting to meeting. It sends the wrong message.

Think of the people you've most admired at work. Do they appear confident? Does it look like they have everything under control? That they are solid, in control, calm, and ready for whatever comes up? Yeah. That's how it *looks*, but the reality is far different. They are no better than you are. Things are crazy. Everything that is happening to you is happening to them. The difference is that they have decided to make it look easy.

In rare cases, it might actually be easy for someone. But that's rare. When a job is easy for someone, they usually get promoted to the point it's no longer easy for them. So, chances are good that the people you are working with are all at the right level to be struggling every day with problems, questions, concerns, deadlines, bosses, turnover, and every other thing you deal with. Make it look easy.

Doing this well starts with accepting the fact that it *can look easy*. It's something you can decide to do. Think about your job. What would it look like if it did look easy? If you were watching yourself do your job, do you look hurried and worried? Or do you look calm and collected? Are you rushing everywhere? Or do you arrive on time and with a smile on your face? Do you have work processes established that allow you to get everything done in the day or do you just "wing it" and hope everything works out?

How you come across to other people is entirely up to you. If you are hurried and worried, is it because you like the drama? Is it because you want everyone to think that you are busy, so you look the part? If so, why? What message are you trying to send? Do you respect a boss or a coworker who looks hurried and worried? If not, why would you expect anyone to respect that behavior *from you*?

Email is not your job.

Don't allow email to control your schedule.

There are going to be exceptions to all of these guidelines. For someone out there reading this, responding to email is your job. But for the rest of us, email is not your job. Check your job description!

Email is the devil. Not only is it notoriously easy to misunderstand email, leading to all kinds of problems at work, but it's a huge waste of time. Most people aren't even reading the email you spend a half-hour crafting. You wasted a tremendous amount of your workday trying to put together the perfect email only to have it end up ignored or skimmed.

There are a lot of little rules that can help you with email organization, and I encourage you to have a system for dealing with your email. But the reality is that we all have a job to do. Your actual job, what you're actually paid to do, has almost nothing to do with email. It's sinister because emails come and go all day long, messages from coworkers, from vendors, inside the organization, outside messages, and the more you engage in reading and responding to those messages, the more you feel like you are doing something. But you're not. Your actual job is not getting done.

In other words, email is giving you that bite-sized, immediate-feedback, dopamine hit on a regular drip all day. Some people like the drama. Or just like to be distracted. They are on mailing lists. They are sending emails about who's going where for lunch. They are signed up for publications and notifications about sales, what the newest thing is that's coming out, or digest emails from forums. Maybe some of the emails you get during your workday are work-related, but I'd be willing to bet that most aren't. 99% of your emails are things you brought on yourself that don't add any value to your actual job. They are just a distraction.

Just like you can waste your entire life looking at cat memes and funny video clips, you can waste your entire career on emails that don't matter. Taking control of your own schedule instead of letting your schedule be defined by your email is a power move with profound impact.

People hear only what they want to hear.

When you communicate with people, keep this principle in mind and it will change every interaction you have. This is the reason why when you give advice, they always seem to screw it up. This is the reason why when you answer a question, they always seem to do what they wanted to do to begin with. This is the reason why you have to repeat yourself.

Even reading this book, you are exemplifying this principle. There are tons of ideas to follow here. Which ideas will stay with you? Almost certainly the ideas that already match up with what you think and believe.

Every argument you've ever had, your words have been twisted and misunderstood because the person you are arguing with hears only what they want to hear. Every book you've ever read, every presentation you've ever sat through, every answer you've ever been given, has all been distorted because of this.

We just aren't very good at hearing things we don't want to hear. If we can avoid dealing with something we don't want to deal with, we will figure out a way. If we can forget something we don't want to remember, we will. Our entire lives are limited by the interactions we have every day, the people we surround ourselves with, the websites, the music, the media. Unless you go out of your way to find something new, you will experience the same things day after day. And guess what? Those things you experience will be the things you like. More of the same.

This makes sense, right? New things might not be as good as old things. We only have so much time in the day, so why risk trying something new when I know I like the old thing. Most of us aren't doing this on purpose. It's the way our lives are structured. We work at the same place, with the same people, doing the same things. We follow the same patterns. And the result is that we only integrate information we receive that fits into this pre-existing framework.

In other words, we only hear what we want to hear.

When you are talking to people at work, trying to get something done, trying to convince or describe, present, impart, or otherwise communicate, remember that the people you are talking to are not hearing everything you are saying. No matter how many times they nod or agree, they are not hearing you. Even if you ask them to echo back what they heard, they will lose the thread moments later. Why? Because unless you can match it up with something they already want to hear, they literally will not hear you.

Most people do not understand what it is supposed to look like.

Most people you work with are well-meaning. They aren't there to cause problems or be malicious. They aren't screwing up on purpose. They come to work *to work*. With that said, most people are making it up as they go. They've never actually seen what it is supposed to look like.

Most people are not good at their jobs. That means most people are learning the job that they have from people who are themselves not very good at their jobs. The examples they follow are not great examples. This creates a situation where mediocre, but well-meaning people demonstrate the job to mediocre, but well-meaning people.

Of course we are going to have problems!

Think about every haircut you've ever gotten, every massage, every server at a restaurant, every doctor visit, car mechanic, landscaper, teacher, or grocery store checker. How many times have you been truly impressed? How many times has someone done their job really *right*? Not just getting the job done, but done with excellence? It's rare. Super-rare.

I think everyone can remember a time when they were blown away by a performance. It's probably more rare that we have the same "blown away" experience from someone that we work with. But even so, some of us are fortunate enough to have had an experience to learn part of our jobs from someone who was really good at it, who put in the time to be great. How did that change your experience of what it meant to do your job?

How many times have you had to sit back and admit to yourself that you have a lot to learn after you see someone else do *your job* better than you?

In many of our jobs, there is a wide range of expectations. Remember, your managers and supervisors are probably not good at their jobs, so they unintentionally aren't clear about what is expected and what a good job is supposed to look like. Employees assume that since they haven't been fired and reprimanded, they must be doing it right. But chances are, they are bumbling through the work day patting themselves on the back without having any idea what a good job actually looks like.

Most people don't understand that they are the problem.

This one comes up a lot in coaching sessions. I'll be talking to the employee about what they are working on and inevitably they start complaining about a process or a person that is stopping them from being successful. I dig deeper, ask questions, get them to open up about what's really going on, and suddenly it becomes very clear that the employee sitting in front of me is the problem. At least, it suddenly becomes clear *to me*. They continue to be blissfully unaware of this fact.

Self-awareness is a rare trait among the people you work with. Most people assume that by showing up and doing their best, they are of course never the problem. It's always someone else that said the wrong thing or did the wrong thing. It's not because they were snarky in an email. It's not because they showed up late to a meeting. It's not because they didn't finish the training course on time. This is a classic problem where we tend to make great excuses for ourselves and assume the worst about everyone else.

When you are working with people, remember that they are stumbling around through the day literally assuming that they are doing every single thing right. They assume that if anything goes wrong, someone else is to blame. They simply do not see that how they interact with other people and how they interact with work processes is causing little (or sometimes big) gaps between actual outcomes and desired outcomes.

Don't get me wrong: People *intend* to do the right thing. They just don't see how what they are doing is the problem. They make allowances for their own behavior in their own minds, but don't extend the same courtesy to everyone else.

The way this manifests is sometimes obvious and sometimes subtle. It can be as simple as reading too much into an email response they received that they perceived as snarky. They forward you the email, ready to complain, and when you read that same email you see that the original message from them was pretty darn blunt. You can see why the other person responded the way they did. But can they see it? No. They can't see it because they know what they meant in the original email, but assumed the worst about the reply.

Of course it's okay for me to be late to work; I ran into traffic; I had to drop off my kids at daycare; the bus was running late; I spilled my coffee on myself and had to go back inside to change. In other words, I was there, so I know why I was late and it was all perfectly innocent and reasonable. But if *you* are late for work, I'm going to assume it was because you are lazy or stupid. I will assume it was to ruin my day, to miss my meeting, or because you are disrespectful of other people's time. The reality is that we are all just living our lives. Point that finger back at yourself.

Nobody cares about your problems.

That's why they are *your problems.*

We all have problems at work, people who are holding up a process, miscommunications, missed deadlines, complications, planning errors, staff turnover, and a million other things that get in the way of what you are trying to accomplish. Remember, all of this *stuff* is part of the job. Of course it would be great if nothing unexpected ever happened, if everyone you talked to understood you perfectly, and if no one ever missed a deadline, but that's not going to happen.

You will be dealing with problems for the rest of your career.

Here's the thing, though: these are *your* problems. And everyone around you has their own problems. Complaining about your problems is not going to get you anywhere. No one cares. They have their own problems to worry about. Sure, you may occasionally run into someone who will listen to your problems, but usually it's only because they want to spew a bunch of half-baked advice your way and pat themselves on the back. You don't need that.

If you report to someone, they don't want to hear about your *problems*. They want to hear about your *solutions*. They understand that not everything is perfect all the time, but spending time complaining about it makes you look delusional or inept. If someone reports to you, complaining to *them* about your problems is downright crazy. Do not do this. You are in a position of authority and they do not care one bit about your problems. Also, do not complain to your coworkers about your problems. You may think that you are humanizing yourself by opening up to them, but you are most-likely coming across as a whiner or someone who cannot handle the job.

It's like going out camping in the summer and complaining that the weather is hot. Of course it's hot! It's the middle of the summer and you are outside! What did you expect? Complaining about your problems at work is no different. Of course you have to deal with problems! You're working with a bunch of people who are not good at their jobs! What did you expect? Keep it to yourself.

If it was easy, it would already be done.

The number of times I hear people talk about how difficult something is borders on outrageous. It's as if "difficult" becomes a reason why we shouldn't do something. That's where I go back to this principle as a reminder that the easy things have all been done. Only the difficult stuff is left to do!

Think about it this way: All of the things that can be done - the easy stuff - *has* been done. The thing you are stuck on, the thing that hasn't been done yet *is the difficult thing to do*. If you find yourself in a conversation and it becomes clear that what you are talking about is how difficult the task, project, or decision is in front of you, that's a good sign. It means that you've done all the easy stuff. The trick is to not get bogged down and focus on the difficulty of the next step. It is *supposed to be difficult*.

I like to think about this like discovering a new species of animal. If everyone already knew about that species of animal, you wouldn't be discovering anything. It would be easy. You would just look it up. But with all the people traveling the world and with all the technology we have for finding things, discovering a new species is by definition difficult. Imagine sitting around complaining about how difficult it would be to find a new species of animal. *Of course it's difficult!* That's not the point. The point is figuring out how to do it.

There is always a finite amount of risk.

People are generally pretty good at identifying reasons why something won't work or reasons why you shouldn't do something. Those same people are generally pretty bad at figuring out how to say yes to something. Using a risk management framework to make decisions can help.

In the universe of risk management, there are only four possible responses to risk:

1) Avoid
2) Transfer
3) Mitigate
4) Accept

That's it. You are an expert on risk management now. Here are some examples of how this works.

Avoid - If there is a way to avoid the problem by changing the plan, that's one option. The problem is that most people avoid the risk by simply saying "no" to it and then nothing gets done.

Transfer - Give the risk to someone else to deal with. A good example is buying insurance. You pay an agreed upon amount while the insurance company takes the risk from you. Your downside is capped at the rate you pay for the insurance, the rest of the risk is transferred to the insurance company.

Mitigate - By all means, figure out ways to reduce the risk of certain outcomes. Have a plan, work a plan. But mitigation doesn't mean not doing it. Mitigation is about figuring out a different way to accomplish the same thing.

Accept - This one throws people for a loop. This is where you identify the risks and then literally accept them for what they are. Acknowledge the negative potential outcomes, understand the impacts, and then go with it.

Risk and Reward are two sides of the same coin.

A Risk Management Framework Conversation:

Them: You can't do this [thing that sounds super risky and terrible to me]!

You: What happens if we do it?

Them: Blahblahblah

You: Wait, let's write each individual outcome down together and make sure we are on the same page about what can happen if we do this. It is important to me that I understand all of the risks you are seeing.

Them: [saying all kinds of crazy things]

You: Okay, is there anything else or do we have everything written down? Actually, it's okay if we missed a few things. This isn't set in stone. But let's use these reasons to get started on our analysis.

For each one of these items you told me about, let's figure out the *probability* and *impact* of the risk event occurring.

For *probability,* tell me about the last time we did this and we had this outcome. Is it something that happens every time? Once per day? Once per year? Have we heard about this happening to anyone else? Is there a business that is famous for this terrible thing happening? Remember, things that happen, "all the time," almost never do.

For *impact*, how much money could we potentially lose if this risk event occurs? Will it put us out of business? That's the worst possible outcome. Will it cost us time (but not money)? Will it impact our reputation or future business? Does it affect a key partnership? Will it get me fired? Remember, the number of risk events that can actually occur that will put us out of business is vanishingly small. Is this one of those risk events?

Okay, we have identified quite a few risks here and assigned an impact and probability to each of them. If we multiply the impact by the probability, we will come up with a risk score for each item that represents the amount of risk each event poses to the business or project. Let's do that.

Based on this list and the scores that resulted, do you feel that we've at least come within range of how much risk we would have if we moved forward with this [thing you don't want to do]? It's not important that it is accurate down to the decimal place, we just need to be in the ballpark.

Them: Yes, I guess so. Wait, I can think of another risk event!

You: Okay, we'll add that one, too. Anything else?

Them: No, I guess not.

You: Great. Thank you for your work on this. I want you to understand that based on this risk analysis, I am *accepting* all of the risk for moving forward with this project. Risk and Reward are two sides of the same coin. By definition, we are going to have to take some measured risks to create the rewards that pay our salaries. We have measured this risk. Part of my role is understanding the risks and moving forward. That's what I am going to do in this situation. I'm asking for your support. Can you get behind this project and help me create another success?

Them: Thank you for hearing me out. Yes, I can support this project.

Most of the time, the person just wants to be heard and understood. They imagine that there is an unlimited amount of risk, which is almost never actually the case. Using a risk management framework to have the conversation removes the argumentative element. It also provides concrete proof, in the form of the written analysis, that risks were identified, categorized, and evaluated. When you conclude that analysis by making it clear that you are accepting the remaining risk, the pressure is off. It's not about opinion or conjecture at that point. Simply ask for support and remind them of the framework whenever there is push-back.

Give the Benefit of the Doubt.

This one is tough for people. It comes from a lack of understanding and a lack of trust. But I see it all the time.

Have you ever been in a meeting where someone suggests an idea and it immediately gets shot down? Sure, that happens. The person who made the original suggestion tries to explain that they've done something like this before and it worked great. But still, the rest of the people aren't interested in moving forward because they can't see how it could possibly work.

Or have you ever found yourself disagreeing with your boss, even though they have more experience and more to lose by making the decision you disagree with? Oh yeah, that happens all the time, too.

Have you ever worked with someone who made a mistake and you're so sure that they did it on purpose to make you look bad, to kill a project, or to push work onto you? I'll bet that's happened to you, too.

In all of these scenarios and many, many more, if you give the benefit of the doubt, you might be surprised how much further you get.

If you doubt someone's skill, experience, or intentions, you've already shut down the possibility of finding new ideas. Instead, if you give the benefit of the doubt, you've opened the door. Your first thought should be *okay, let's see where this goes*.

Have excellent conversations.

In some jobs, you're talking with folks all day long. In other jobs, you may only be talking with folks at certain meetings. But whatever it is, conversations can be a big part of what you are doing.

If you're going to have conversations, have *excellent* conversations.

The reality is that we have a lot of mediocre conversations. We have conversations that don't mean much, that make no impact. We sometimes even tear each other down. But every once in a while you'll walk away from a conversation and it will be remarkable.

That was a good conversation.

You'll be glad you had the conversation. You will have learned something. You will have made a connection or found an opportunity. Because of the conversation, things will have *changed*.

Those are excellent conversations. Those are the conversations you want to have.

Here's the secret: You have control over if a conversation is excellent.

Think about your last *excellent* conversation. What made it excellent? Now, be the person that creates the excellent conversation for someone else!

Give them a way out.

Some people pride themselves on backing people into a corner. They deliver ultimatums. This even works sometimes. But this almost never works long-term. Eventually, it catches up with you.

What happens is that you maneuver people into a position where they can't get out. Except there are always two solutions to a problem. And if the only other option is to quit, your ultimatum starts to look silly when the person simply says, "no."

There will be times in your career when you take a clear position on something: Take it or leave it. In rare circumstances, this might even make sense. It's certainly clear. But be prepared when the other person decides to take the 'leave it" option. Most of the time, you should give the other person a way out.

This is especially important for any ongoing relationship. Your coworkers. Your boss. Your team. Even if you are leaving the organization, you never know where you'll be in the future. You've heard the phrase, "don't burn your bridges." There are moments when you've crossed the bridge and the can of gas is in your hand. You might even have the matches lit. And you have a decision to make. But more often than not, the situation is not as clear.

You're burning bridges a little at a time and don't even know it.

A great example of this is asking your boss for a raise. If you're doing this right, it shouldn't be a complete surprise to your boss. The meeting should be thought-out. You should be able to explain what you are doing to contribute to the organization and how you will continue to provide value. You should have a good sense of comparable positions inside and outside your organization along with comparable compensation and benefits. But even if you get all of that right, where people get stuck is delivering an ultimatum.

Based on all of my research and my contributions at this organization, I'm asking for a 20% raise.

Now what is your boss going to do? Don't leave it up to chance.

Instead, give them a way out.

And when I say give them a way out, I do not mean to say, "or don't give me a raise, that's okay, too." It's not about giving them an easy door to walk through, it's about creating space to work.

Based on all of my research and my contributions at this organization, I'm asking how we can work together to revise my current job description or put me in a new position to achieve as much as a 20% pay increase over the next 6 months. At that point, I'd appreciate the opportunity to evaluate my performance in the new position and keep my original performance evaluation date 6 months after that to be considered for another pay increase.

Your boss can work with that. It gives room. It builds bridges. It demonstrates understanding that the organization can seldom flip a switch and make wholesale changes to compensation or just about anything else.

Find the edges so you can find the middle.

There's a quick way to figure out where everyone stands on a topic: suggest absurd things.

This is a concept carried over from risk management, but it works in many areas of your organization. Basically, there are limits or edges to what can be done. Sometimes those limits are way further out than you first expect.

It's a natural tendency for people to immediately try to find a consensus. This approach limits possibilities and puts the focus on trying to convince everyone to agree with a certain position. Instead, take the opportunity to push the boundaries. Find the edges.

Here's a simple example. Let's say you are selling your house. You need to set a price. How much money do you want for your house?

Most people will start down the path of looking up comparable house prices or checking for an automated valuation. But really think about it. What am I asking you?

The answer is that you want infinite money for your house. You want all the money. You want to set the price so high that it causes computers to crash. You want a price so high that we use up all the numbers and need to start making up new ways to do math.

What's the lowest price you would accept for your house?

Again, you might start by saying that you wouldn't sell the house for less than what you own on the mortgage. But is that really what I'm asking you?

You could give your house away. You could *pay someone* to take your house from you.

How useful is this exercise? You'd be surprised. With a house, the price will be what the market will pay. You just need to decide if you are willing to accept the market price for the house to sell it. But with many projects at work, what you are actually deciding is not so clear. There may not be a market yet for the product you are developing. It may be an internal project designed to increase efficiency. It may be an entirely new strategy for your business line. Whatever it is, don't miss the opportunity to find the edges, the true edges.

Once you find the edges, it's very simple to find the middle.

Execute is in the name!

Executives execute. Directors direct. Managers manage.

For many people, these titles and terms are fuzzy. They all run together. And it makes it difficult to understand the role that any one position plays at an organization. When people take on different roles, they often bring this confusion along with them and things start to get out of order.

So, let's take a look at how this works.

Directors, as in *The Board of Directors*, direct the CEO and Executives to translate guidance statements into strategic execution. Directors set long-term goals and hire the right CEO to realize those goals.

Executives execute. The CEO and Executive team define and implement strategies to turn guidance statements into something that can actually be accomplished.

Managers manage. The manager is the person who makes the day-to-day activities of the business happen as planned. They are often the people who are breaking the strategies into actionable pieces and working with teams to integrate and adapt current processes as needed to bring the strategies to life.

Think of it this way. Work can be divided into a few different categories. Fixing stuff that's broken. Doing stuff as designed. Doing stuff we've never done before.

When things are supposed to happen a certain way but for whatever reason they don't happen that way, someone has to fix it. It could be a process that wasn't followed properly. Or a machine that breaks down. Or an error in your system. Whatever it is, a surprisingly large amount of the work that we do is to correct a problem. It's a combination of fixing the error now and fixing the error for the future.

But most work is just doing whatever is supposed to be done the way it is supposed to be done. If you build something, most work is just building that thing. If you process documents, most of the time you will just be processing documents. If you take orders, most of the time you'll be taking orders. There are entire departments or teams that just do whatever they do all day, every day.

Some work is doing new things. Automating a process. Changing a tool. Updating a procedure. Finding efficiency in a workflow. Implementing a new platform. Whatever it is, some amount of the work that we do is to do something we've never done before.

The World is a Big Place.

It sure is.

Everything you've ever done. Every thought you've ever had. Every place you've ever gone. It's all happened before to someone else.

You might be in the vanishingly small percentage of people who over the course of your entire life has done something truly new. Maybe. But I doubt it. Odds are that every moment of your entire life has been experienced by someone else throughout the course of human history.

Sure, there's only one of you. And you are a unique person experiencing the world in your own unique way. I won't take that away from you. But if you zoom out a bit, we're all sharing experiences with someone, somewhere, throughout the fullness of time.

I find that comforting.

And if you think about work in that context, you'll see that you are not alone. This is why coaching, and mentoring, and communication are so important. But that's not what this is about.

What this is about is that the world is a big place with a lot of people in it. And a lot of them are doing the same thing you are doing at work. Maybe not at your company, but somewhere in the world people are doing your job.

It's easy to focus on yourself in meetings, presentations, conversations with coworkers, projects, reports, performance evaluations, emails, and phone calls. Those frustrations of your job that hold you back, those concerns and worries that keep you up at night, just remember that the world is a big place.

Yes, there is only one of you and it feels like the world is on your shoulders alone. But it's not. The world is way, way too big to be on your shoulders alone.

Ideas are easy. Execution is difficult.

Hey, I've got a great idea! People say that all the time. *You've* said it.

And maybe you did have a great idea. Not every idea is great, but there are a lot of great ideas out there. I can come up with a hundred great ideas before I get out of the shower in the morning.

That's not the difficult part.

Execution is the difficult part. Turning ideas into reality is where things become challenging.

During the course of your work day, ideas will occur to you that you may not be able to put into action. Maybe it's because it would take resources you don't control. Time, money, priorities, and coordinated effort are required to make your ideas real.

At some point in your life, you've worked to make an idea real. It could have been a project at work, something you did for a charity, or when you were part of a team. We all understand how this works.

And yet…

The number of times I talk to people who are convinced they have great ideas and just haven't been given the chance to execute them is alarmingly high. No one wants to hear that coming up with the idea is the easy part. I give away great ideas all the time. Why? Because I know that the hard part is turning that idea into something real.

By all means, confidently share your great ideas. But understand that speaking the idea into the world is not what's stopping you from seeing that idea become a reality. Although the idea is the important spark, it's the engine of execution you need to keep running if you want to make the idea into something real.

There's always a #1 concern.

During the course of your career as an employee, team-member, manager, or executive, there will always be "concerns." You can think of this as complaints, problems, or issues. There are lots of ways to describe the same thing, but it all boils down to setting priorities.

But this isn't about setting priorities.

This is about realizing that no matter what you do, no matter how many tickets you close or complaints you resolve, no matter how many problems you address or issues you resolve, there will always be a list. And the list will always have a #1.

I've been in many planning sessions and department meetings where it is clear that the group believes that there is a future where none of these complaints, problems, or issues will exist. If only we do this and that just right, it will all go away. Then we can focus on the *real work*! But that's not actually how it works.

It's clear that it isn't how it actually works because every one of us starts every workday with a list of complaints, problems, and issues. And there's always something at the top of that list.

I'm not saying that we shouldn't work to resolve these things. In fact, resolving these things may be the thing you were hired to do. What I'm saying is that there is something liberating to shift your view and to understand that there will always be something at the top of that list.

Understanding, managing, and planning for how to handle *that list* is a necessary byproduct of having responsibility. When you no longer have the responsibility, you will no longer have the list. But someone else will!

Offer to help.

You'd be surprised at how many opportunities to learn something new, advance your career, or contribute to something meaningful come from simply offering to help.

As with many things in this book, the suggestion of "offer to help," sounds obvious. Yet, when I talk to employees during coaching sessions, I rarely hear that they've offered to help. They want everything that comes along with helping: meeting new people, learning new things, creating value. But do they offer to help? No.

When was the last time you genuinely offered to help at work?

It's as if people are expecting an invitation. Everyone assumes the same things that you do. They assume you are too busy to help. They assume that you wouldn't want to help. They assume that it's more work for them if you help because you don't know what you are doing. In other words, you can't sit back and expect an invite.

But before you offer to help, be truly effective at your current job. Be great! Once you have everything in order, your best opportunity for growth and visibility is to offer to help. Take on a new project. Join a new team. Sit in on a meeting from another area.

Don't fall into the trap of offering to help and getting everything dumped on you. Set some ground rules for yourself. Only commit to the things you know you can deliver. Produce fantastic results. Start small, execute, and get into the habit of offering to help.

We fill our days.

Every moment of every day, you spend doing something. It could be that you spend some of the time doing nothing, but that's still something. Something moves each moment forward. Day turns into night. Night turns into day.

This happens whether you want it to or not. This happens inevitably. And this happens to everyone.

I could tell you that you need to seize the moment. I could tell you that you need to fill every day with excitement and passion and learning and doing. And those would be good things. But you already know all of that.

That's not what this is.

You spend every moment at work doing something. So does everyone else. And you have a tremendous amount of control over how you spend those moments. So does everyone else. At some point in your career, you'll slip into a mode where you are "counting the minutes." Maybe you have somewhere to be after work, so you can't wait for the day to be over. Maybe you are meeting someone for lunch that you haven't seen in a while, so the morning feels like it is dragging on. When this happens, you aren't in the moment. You are living for another time.

Think of this like borrowing happiness from tomorrow.

People do this all the time. They also borrow worry from tomorrow. Either way, you can only live in the moment you're in. And that's just as true at work as it is every other moment of your day.

This might seem obvious. Of course people fill up their day with moments. But think about your work day. Think about it moment to moment. How much of that time is you just moving along, focused on something happening later or tomorrow? Or worse, just "killing time," until you can do something else?

You can only be in one place at any given moment. Make the most of it. Don't fast-forward.

Things get better when you make them get better.

Have you ever heard of entropy?

Entropy is a sciency word that has a sciency meaning, but the concept of entropy has a profound possibility to impact every part of your life. Basically, entropy says that things don't become more orderly on their own. Things naturally become less orderly.

Now think about your own life and your own work. Do things get better and better on their own? No. It takes *work* to make things better. We put energy into whatever it is we are working on and *that's* how it gets better.

If you don't clean off your desk every night, what happens? The coffee mug from yesterday is still sitting there. Maybe there's a pen or two rolled under some papers. Crumbs from your lunch are spilled and brushed to the side. Your phone is dusty because you always use the headset instead of the handset. Your monitor has smudges on it. Little by little, your desk becomes disorderly.

Most people don't see this happening. Every once in a while, something catastrophic happens that triggers a thorough cleaning. Usually, it's a big spill. Coffee everywhere! Suddenly, cleaning off your desk becomes a high priority. So, you spend time and effort (work) to make your desk more orderly. When you put in work, you create order. That's how we literally work *against* entropy.

Now think about not your messy desk, but your messy work. If you stopped doing your work, some things would fall apart almost immediately. Other things would take longer to fall apart. But it would eventually all fall apart. That's entropy. It's constantly working against you. Your work, no matter what it is, is bringing order to chaos. By putting in the work, you are making things better!

This applies to everything from updating a spreadsheet to inventing a new system. Your work is what makes things better. And it doesn't happen unless you do it. Things get better when you make them get better.

Don't manufacture drama.

There's enough drama without you adding to it.

I can see it now, you're reading this thinking, "I don't manufacture drama!" Oh? Is that right? Let's see.

Crisis management is like a drug. In a crisis, things are clear. People understand that immediate action is needed to avert the crisis. Teams typically respond well to crisis situations. Leaders emerge. Sure, eggs get broken along the way, but that's how we make omelets! There is a pressing need and an immediacy that cuts through the ho-hum. Feedback becomes much more immediate. And people get recognized for "handling the crisis."

I'll bet that sounds familiar.

Every once in a while, there will be a genuine crisis. And the team really will need to manage out of that crisis to be successful. But that should be rare. Unless you work in emergency services, most day-to-day jobs are not supposed to be a crisis.

Why?

Because in almost every job, you have the ability to plan for the future. The future isn't happening to you. *You are happening to it.* A crisis means that something has gone horribly wrong. You're off track and off plan.

Here's where the drama comes in.

Being "on plan" is boring. If you do it right, it doesn't even feel difficult or challenging because, well, everything is going according to plan. That is how it is *supposed to feel*. But there's no rush. No crisis. No drama.

So what happens? People make it up. They make drama happen. They spin stories. They stir things up. They throw things off. They get off plan. It happens every day all around you. And if you have been praised in the past for handling a "tough situation," you can easily fall into the trap of manufacturing more of those "tough situations."

Drama can take mana forms, but personnel issues to project roadblocks. But now that I've pointed it out, you'll see it. If you are involved in some drama at work, consider where it came from. Is it truly a crisis? Or is it all made up?

Your words coming out of their mouths.

I love this one. I love it because one of the difficult things about leadership is knowing when it starts working. But when you start to hear what you've been saying coming from the people you work with, you know the message is making it through.

Remember to repeat yourself. Why? Because most people aren't listening. It's not that they don't want to listen, it's that they can't. Listening is difficult. There are distractions. They are busy. It takes practice. But more than that, it takes a long time for someone to internalize a concept. So, repeat yourself.

If you repeat yourself enough, what you say will start to "click." And you'll hear it click because people will literally parrot your own words back to you or to each other. This is uncanny to experience.

There's a super-weird part of this that you just need to accept and get over. In almost every case, the person saying your words will not remember that you said them. They will insist that they came up with it themselves. That's not a bad thing. It means that they have fully internalized the concept and are now ready to take the message to other people.

When your words are coming out of the mouths of the people you work with, you know that the work you are doing is making an impact.

Every job has a purpose.

Most of us don't think about the true purpose of our job. But there is one. There's a reason that your job exists. It's not just to get the work in front of us done, but it is to move something forward or keep something in place. We're fighting against entropy.

For some jobs, the purpose is crystal clear. Some jobs even have purpose statements. Think of the Police officers who "protect and serve." The purpose is right there. You put on the badge, you know what you are expected to do.

Do you know what your job's purpose is?

And if you do, are you fulfilling it?

If I asked you right now to write down a purpose statement for your job, could you do it? Try it. Your purpose statement should be short. It should be clear. It should be concise. Other people who do your job should be able to read it and nod in agreement. You should be able to say it to your coworkers and it will resonate.

> *My job as the CEO is to ensure that the company is executing the strategic plan.*

That's it. Full stop. Everything else that comes up had better be supporting the execution of the strategic plan. There will be personnel issues, financial plans, risk assessments, audits, politics, information security, and a million other things to *manage*, but the purpose of my job doesn't change.

I challenge you to define your purpose. Once you have your purpose clearly defined, I challenge you to consider what you do every day. Does it match with what you should be doing?

When you get what you want, stop talking.

You've heard this one before, but you haven't really heard it.

I know you haven't heard it because it never fails that when someone should have stopped talking, they just keep going.

Look, there's a lot of negotiation in your work. It may not be as clear as a contract negotiation or asking for a raise, but you are likely negotiating things all day long. It could be something you are working on with a person on your team. It could be work with another department or manager. It could be a deal you are putting together for a client. Negotiating takes many forms.

I've seen some spectacular negotiations fall apart *after the deal was made* because the person just keeps on talking. This is natural. When you feel like you are winning, you start celebrating. In a negotiation, celebrating means you just keep talking. And in some cases, you talk yourself out of whatever you just talked yourself into.

The best way to practice this is to listen to other people. This is great fun in meetings of all types. Listen to what is being said and take note of when someone should have stopped talking. If you listen for it, you will hear it. Then see if they keep talking. They almost always will.

If you ask a question like, "do we agree?" and the answer is, "yes!", stop talking.

Something always has to give.

Welcome to the world of logic and reason where everything makes sense. Ha!

You are a hard worker, right? You fill your day with the work that you need to do for everything to get done. You spend time outside of work to learn and grow and change. You meet people. You have a family. You attend events.

You are busy.

Each and every minute of every single day is full of *something*. It might not all be measurable or productive, but you are certainly spending every minute doing things.

So, when you decide to do something new, something has to give.

I mean this literally. You need to give something up to do something new.

Most of the time what happens is that people take on something new and try to a schedule that is - by definition - already full. You already have a full time job. You are working on stuff full time. Doing something new means something on the list of things you are already doing is not going to get done.

This sounds obvious, right? And yet, I see it all the time. The new thing gets added, nothing else gets subtracted, and then things start to go downhill. Because of course they do! Something has to give.

Let's say that you are living your life right now. You're filling your day with things. Then suddenly you decide that you are going to start taking the karate classes you always wanted to. Great! What are you doing to *stop* doing to make that work?

Have you ever asked that question?

If you are like everyone else, you probably haven't considered it. You sign up for the karate classes and try to make it work. Everything suffers. You get burned out. And then life *forces* you to quit something.

This outcome is *avoidable*. It requires you to make choices.

The same thing happens at work. Your day is full. Your boss asks you to take on a new project. Your next step is to provide your boss with a list of items that you do and ask which one they want you to stop doing!

If that sounds too bold for you, instead ask your boss to talk through a list of priorities with you and to place the new item on the list. Then ask about the items on the bottom of the list. "If the lowest priority items at the bottom of the list didn't get done, would we be significantly impacted?" Make the conversation clear that you want to get everything done, but that adding new items without taking items away is unreasonable. Something has to give.

Be the shadow, then be the light.

We are surrounded every day by learning opportunities. People are telling us things, sometimes unintentionally, sometimes by actions instead of words, but it's happening all the time. Observation is a powerful tool.

Whenever you are in a new situation, be the shadow. Allow yourself to be taught. Ask for mentorship. Ask for a demonstration. Be open to what is being given to you. Your intentionality is what will set you apart from everyone else.

Even the best of us usually stop right there.

Why? Because being the light is really, really difficult.

Once you've learned something, your new role is to teach it. Look for opportunities to teach and show and demonstrate. Your intentionality is what will set you apart from everyone else.

This can be as simple as asking, "Do you want me to show you how to do this?"

You will be surprised how often this simple question works. It makes you more valuable. Showing someone how to do what you do forces you to really understand it. Communicating what you do to someone else is different than doing it. A lot of people can do what they do. Few people can explain how they do it.

Be the light.

Braces make your teeth straight.

Braces do not make your teeth whiter, bigger, smaller, or cleaner. No amount of flossing, brushing, or polishing will make your teeth straighter.

With teeth, this is obvious. You can (and should!) spend time keeping your teeth clean. You can even spend extra time making your teeth whiter. You can practice smiling. You can do a lot of things on your own. But what you can't do is make your teeth straighter. To get straighter teeth, you need something to push on your teeth and move them to where they need to be.

Guess what? Your work is like that, too. There are a lot of things you can do on your own. Training and practice and meetings and reading and everything else. But to really move in the right direction, you need someone pushing you to where you need to be.

Get a mentor.

Get two!

Do what it takes to reach out to people who can push you and help you change. This person could be your boss, but probably isn't. This person might not even work at the company where you work. Your mentor can help you in ways that you can't help yourself.

Do everything you can to keep your teeth clean, but remember that almost everyone needs braces to have straight teeth.

Most people don't do the thing they are good at...

...because most of the time they do other things.

Over the course of an entire day, many things are competing for our attention. Everything from taking a shower in the morning to making a quick lunch to cleaning up a spilled drink is happening and happening and happening.

Do you know what's not happening most of the time? The thing you are good at.

I might be reasonably good at making food. I might even be a trained chef with a restaurant. I might make food every single night for a restaurant full of satisfied customers. But on the whole, I still spend most of the day doing things *other than making food*.

You can use any example you want here. Think about your own life. You have a skill or a talent. It might even be something valuable. It might even be your job to perform this skill on a regular basis. Even in the best of circumstances you spend most of your time *not doing the thing you are good at*.

And so does everyone else.

Most of the time, you are not seeing people at their best. You might even be seeing them at their worst. Even at work, most of the time you are not seeing people at their best.

Think of an obvious example. You go to see a brilliant pianist in concert. You watch and listen to this person play the piano for several hours. It's amazing. You are seeing this person at their best. What you are not seeing is the countless hours that this person spent doing everything else in their life. And I'm not just talking about practicing playing the piano. I'm talking about this person brushing their teeth. Taking out the trash. Having an argument over something silly.

You are that person, too.

A full life is important. Don't short-change yourself on experience. But! As much as possible, structure the time you spend working to spend the maximum time doing the thing you are great at. Identify what that is and take note of your work day. How much time do you spend doing the thing that makes you great?

Effort does not get results.

It seems like it should, right? The harder we work, the more we should have to show for it. But it rarely works this way. You've heard before that it isn't just practice that matters, it's practice with a purpose. And that's right. Purposeful practice makes a dramatic difference in whatever you are working to achieve.

And yet, we easily fall into the trap of focusing on effort (and not results).

She's trying. He's trying. We're all trying. Trying is the bare minimum. Of course you are trying. But you're not paid to try. You're paid to produce results.

It's easy to recognize and even to reward effort. As you lead and supervise, don't be tempted. You'll have many opportunities to say, "at least you tried," or, "great effort," or, "you'll get it next time." It's encouraging to say these things. Sometimes people need that. But better feedback is, "I see you worked hard on this, but here's where you need to focus."

Bring the conversation back to the goal.

What worked yesterday won't work tomorrow.

Change is inevitable. We see it all around us. Just when you get used to something, it changes. There have been countless books written about change, and yet this is something that almost everyone forgets.

We forget about it because it's easier to ignore it. When you find something that works, it's easier to settle in. We all remember hearing, "if it ain't broke don't fix it," at some point in our lives. And while that may be true from time to time, changing things to make them better is how we innovate and differentiate and all the other words that rhyme.

In many coaching sessions with employees, the conversation will come around to something about how things "used to work." And because it used to work that way, it's tough to accept that it just won't work that way today.

Maybe the company outgrew the technology or (gulp) even the employee who "used to" do whatever you're talking about today. Things change. Markets change. Consumers change. Demands and designs change. And they change whether we want them to or not.

Guess what? Those same things are going to change tomorrow, too. The things you are doing today aren't going to work anymore. You either need to change the things you are doing or, well, you won't be doing them anyway because you'll be out of business or out of a job.

In other words, be the thing that is happening *to* the change. Not the other way around. If you accept that the change is going to happen and that what you are doing today isn't going to work tomorrow, why wait for things to change? Change it yourself.

There's a difference between blame and responsibility.

We get defensive when something goes wrong. This is especially true when it isn't our fault! There's nothing worse than being blamed for something that isn't our fault.

Except…

Well, except that if you manage or lead people or projects, things are going to go wrong. And when things go wrong, you're going to get blamed for them.

Except…

Are you really being blamed? The truth is that most of the time your boss and your team aren't blaming you for whatever went wrong. It's not about you. It's not about what you could have done differently to avoid whatever went wrong. Remember, you're supposed to be taking risks as long as you understand the risk.

What's actually happening is that your boss is expecting you to take *responsibility* for whatever went wrong. This has nothing to do with blame.

I often hear, "It's not my fault," or, "there's nothing I could have done." Great. That's not the issue. The Issue is that something went wrong on your project or with your team and it's your *responsibility* to fix it. Your job is to provide a solution. The blame is irrelevant because the problem already exists and needs to be solved.

As leaders, people on your team will make mistakes. Things won't go quite right. And when things do go wrong, it may not be your fault but it is your responsibility. When you feel that you are to blame for something, especially something that it's your fault, it's easy to become defensive and focus on shifting the blame to someone else. That almost never works. What does work is accepting responsibility and offering solutions.

Be the Boss You Wish You Had

Build Relationships
Meet Regularly
Educate Yourself
Share Knowledge
Coach
Mentor
Plan for Succession

Imagine the perfect boss. Who is this person? Does the perfect boss connect people to each other? Are they generous with knowledge and skills? Do they share what they know for the benefit of the team and the company? Do they lift people up and give opportunities? Do they communicate often about what's going on?

That sounds about right.

In fact, I'd be willing to bet that if you worked for someone who did all of these things, you'd feel a steady, day-by-day improvement in your abilities. You'd automatically learn and grow and change and accomplish more than you ever thought possible.

You'd turn into a superhero.

Now, imagine the worst boss. Who is this person? Do they keep you in the dark? Do they take credit for your hard work? Is it impossible to get the support and information you need to be successful? Are they distant and unfocused? Do they not seem to know what's going on?

That sounds about right.

Don't be that person. It's simple to not be that person. Just because it's simple doesn't mean it's easy. But it is possible to be the boss everyone wishes that they had. This is your opportunity to *be that boss* for other people.

Build Relationships. Connect the dots for people. Not everyone needs to be your friend. And not everyone needs to be friends with each other. But people and teams who have real connections are able to push aside complications and get things done when they otherwise wouldn't. Your company is not a collection of buildings and computers and policies. It's people! You don't need to be a party planner, but you do need to bring people together. Look for work-related interests that connect departments together. Set people from different areas to work on a task. They learn the thing they are working on *and* learn about each other in the process.

Meet Regularly. It's team-building and problem-solving in a one-two punch. Plus, it helps to form good habits. A routine is important and efficient. Remember, if no one is running the meeting, you run the meeting!

Educate Yourself. Keep learning. Read a book. Most of you will have taken specialized training or courses to learn what you know about your job. If you're a medical doctor, you went to medical school. If you are an engineer, you learned a lot of math. Why would leadership be any different? Learning about leadership is like any other skill. Set up a reading group with other leaders. Talk about successes. Talk about failures! Invite people to hold you accountable for achieving your goals. Don't think of the books you read or the courses you take as instructions. It really doesn't matter what they are saying. They are designed to get you thinking about your own leadership and management process.

Share Knowledge. You rock. Figure out why and share it. It makes your job *easier*. And it builds up your team. Make presentations. Write papers. Even if there's no one there to see your presentation or read your paper, taking the time to create these things will fortify your knowledge. You might be surprised who notices.

Coach. Regular coaching helps with performance reviews. Not only are they better reviews overall, but the reviews write themselves! Everyone already knows what's going to happen. No surprises. Nothing should ever be a surprise on a performance evaluation. Ask lots of questions during coaching sessions. Show genuine interest in the success of the people you work with! People already know what they are supposed to do. Your job is to get them to say it and understand what it means.

Mentor. Mentoring is not coaching. Coaching is showing someone how to do *their* job. Mentoring is showing someone how to do *your* job. You've gotten to where you are. Mentoring is your chance to help someone else do the same.

Plan for Succession. There needs to be someone to hand your job off to. Why? So that you can go do the next big thing! Planning your replacement is part of your job. That's part of what you are doing as a leader. If I were to ask you who will replace you when you are promoted and you're not sure of the answer, you're doing something wrong.

In other words, don't be an idiot!

Be the boss you wish you had.

www.ingramcontent.com/pod-product-compliance
Lightning Source LLC
Chambersburg PA
CBHW060830220526
45466CB00003B/1053